MW00562741

"As an advocate for relational approaches to spirituality, I am extremely grateful to Strawn and Brown for their profoundly intelligent and practical insights in *Enhancing Christian Life*. They have extended my understanding of the relational, social, and embodied nature of spirituality. This book has me reflecting in fresh ways on all kinds of things, ranging from theories of human nature to the dynamics of psychotherapy practice to the purpose of checking my cellphone while waiting in line at the grocery store. This is the best book I have read connecting neuroscience, psychology, and the day-to-day realities of spiritual formation."

Steven J. Sandage, Albert and Jessie Danielsen Professor of Psychology of Religion and Theology, Boston University School of Theology

"Want to be a more Christian Christian? Read this book and put its lessons into practice within your church and family. Brad D. Strawn and Warren S. Brown, in *Enhancing Christian Life*, have caught a new, transformative way of understanding Christian formation. They base Christian formation on modern cognitive psychology that recognizes how intertwined relationships are with our embodied life. What they contribute is a thorough description of the Christian implications of this relational approach for the church and Christian relationships. Their book will make you want to engage more with the church. By doing so, both you and the church will be blessed."

Everett L. Worthington Jr., author of *Forgiving and Reconciling*

"In case you were under the impression that being a Christian is a solo achievement, Brad Strawn and Warren Brown are here to disabuse you of that misunderstanding. They say it's a mistake to assume that spirituality is ever an individual, internal, and private matter. For them, it is always an embodied, collective, and spatial enterprise. Written in a lively, down-to-earth fashion, this book has monumental implications for our understanding of both spirituality and ecclesiology."

Michael Frost, author of *Incarnate* and *To Alter Your World*

"This book is a timely wake-up call for the church in this generation to remember that the church is 'a group of followers of Christ who understand themselves as embodied, engaged, enacting, and extending into one another's lives for the sake of the world and the glory of God.' These basic truths are presented with a new freshness and relevance as the authors draw heavily on 'the theory of embodied cognition.' They are well-informed and reliable guides to fresh insights from this cutting-edge theory in cognitive psychology."

Malcolm Jeeves, professor emeritus and past president of the Royal Society of Edinburgh, Scotland's National Academy

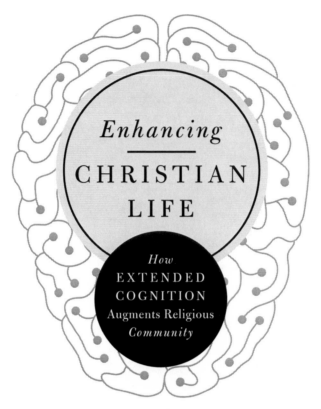

Enhancing

CHRISTIAN LIFE

How
EXTENDED
COGNITION
Augments Religious
Community

BRAD D. STRAWN

•

WARREN S. BROWN

ivp
Academic
An imprint of InterVarsity Press
Downers Grove, Illinois

InterVarsity Press
P.O. Box 1400, Downers Grove, IL 60515-1426
ivpress.com
email@ivpress.com

©2020 by Warren S. Brown and Brad D. Strawn

*All rights reserved. No part of this book may be reproduced in any form without written permission from
InterVarsity Press.*

*InterVarsity Press® is the book-publishing division of InterVarsity Christian Fellowship/USA®, a movement of students
and faculty active on campus at hundreds of universities, colleges, and schools of nursing in the United States of America,
and a member movement of the International Fellowship of Evangelical Students. For information about local and
regional activities, visit intervarsity.org.*

*All Scripture quotations, unless otherwise indicated, are taken from The Holy Bible, New International Version®, NIV®.
Copyright © 1973, 1978, 1984, 2011 by Biblica, Inc.™ Used by permission of Zondervan. All rights reserved worldwide.
www.zondervan.com. The "NIV" and "New International Version" are trademarks registered in the United States Patent
and Trademark Office by Biblica, Inc.™*

*While any stories in this book are true, some names and identifying information may have been changed to protect the
privacy of individuals.*

Cover design and image composite: Faceout Studio
Interior design: Daniel van Loon

ISBN 978-0-8308-5281-9 (print)
ISBN 978-0-8308-2840-1 (digital)

Printed in the United States of America ∞

*InterVarsity Press is committed to ecological stewardship and to the conservation of natural resources in all our
operations. This book was printed using sustainably sourced paper.*

Library of Congress Cataloging-in-Publication Data
A catalog record for this book is available from the Library of Congress.

| **P** | 25 | 24 | 23 | 22 | 21 | 20 | 19 | 18 | 17 | 16 | 15 | 14 | 13 | 12 | 11 | 10 | 9 | 8 | 7 | 6 | 5 | 4 | 3 | 2 | 1 |
| **Y** | 41 | 40 | 39 | 38 | 37 | 36 | 35 | 34 | 33 | 32 | 31 | 30 | 29 | 28 | 27 | 26 | 25 | 24 | 23 | 22 | 21 | 20 |

CONTENTS

ACKNOWLEDGMENTS

A PREMISE OF THIS BOOK is that what we tend to attribute to ourselves—our own minds and intellects, as well as our Christian lives—is in reality thoughts, ideas, characteristics, capacities, and conceptual structures that have been contributed to us by others. As was true of our previous book, *The Physical Nature of Christian Life*, the ideas that have gone into this book were themselves supersized by ideas we encountered in reading the books of others, and in discussions with colleagues, students, and friends. We are grateful to have had the privilege of being nested in such a rich environment of thoughts and ideas.

Both of us are products of academic and professional life histories that have significantly influenced our thinking about the topics in this book. In the acknowledgments to our previous book we took time to recognize the important persons and ideas that are part of our particular histories. However, beyond these general historical influences, there are specific persons and books that have been our guides (and goads) throughout the writing of this book.

We have been particularly influenced by the writings of philosopher Andy Clark, as will be evident in the frequency with which he is cited in this book. Clark's ideas about intelligence and mind form the core of our exposition of the nature of Christian life. Other books that have contributed to our thinking are listed in the bibliography at the back of this book.

Our colleague Kutter Callaway, from Fuller's School of Theology, was kind enough to read a previous draft of this book and provide valuable feedback that prompted us to make improvements in the presentation of our thoughts. Fuller theology graduate student Nicole Jones also read the previous draft and gave much-needed feedback, particularly with respect to our analysis of

Christian religious experiences. Reverend Tara Beth Leach took time from her role as lead pastor and author to provide a helpful pastoral perspective. Dennis Vogt, a well-read friend and person who thinks deeply about the church and Christian life, gave valuable feedback at several points along the way that has significantly influenced our thoughts. Finally, we are indebted to Jon Boyd, editorial director at IVP Academic, for his very helpful and insightful suggestions for revisions to this book.

HIDDEN FIGURES

Perhaps the greatest scientific and engineering achievement of the latter part of the twentieth century was the US space program—the earth orbits of Mercury and Gemini, and the moon orbits and landings of Apollo. We have all seen videos of (or remember watching live) the launches at Cape Canaveral, scenes of activity in the flight control room, and the first steps of Neil Armstrong on the moon. The whole scenario was a huge intellectual and engineering achievement that so obviously could not have been accomplished by a single individual or even a small group. Success required a huge network of persons interacting with one another, sharing the outcomes of their scientific and engineering work, and using the tools available to enhance their mental capacities for the complex work of the project.

As depicted in the movie *Hidden Figures*, a group of expert African American female mathematicians served as "human computers" on NASA space projects, prior to the availability of electronic digital computers. Extensive and complex calculations that the engineers and scientists needed were given to this group. The cognitive processes of the scientists were therefore extended and enhanced by the work of these women, allowing the scientists to concentrate on broader issues. However, the work of these women was hidden, both in the sense that they were cloistered away in the basement of another building, and in the sense that their work was taken for granted by the engineers and scientists of the project. The racial inequities and injustices inherent in this whole sad scenario is a central theme of the movie. Nevertheless, this story clearly illustrates what we wish to discuss in this book. The NASA scientists and engineers relied heavily on these women to extend and complete the mental processes involved in their scientific work. However, as is human nature, they presumed that the value and contribution of the calculations these women completed were attributable solely to their own intellectual achievements. The degree to which the women extended and enhanced their mental work was hidden.

Philosopher of mind Andy Clark argues that none of us are as smart as we think we are, particularly if you strip away the things outside of us that enhance our capacities—the tools we use, the intellectual leverage gained from interactions with other persons, and the contributions to our thinking of the accumulated history of the work of others. In so many ways our cognitive abilities are significantly enhanced by our ability to *extend* our current mental processing networks to *include* available tools, other persons, and the knowledge, skills, and practices that make up our particular field of work.

This book is about the hidden figures of Christian life. Our premise is that when we strip away the contributions of others, particularly those within our local body of believers, we are not as spiritual as we believe ourselves to be. We presume that our spirituality and Christian life are attributable to us as individuals. But within the life networks of all Christians are hidden figures that allow and enhance our Christian living—at least this is true and necessary, we will argue, with respect to the richest and most robust Christian living.

EXTENDING CHRISTIAN LIFE

"*I* am not Christian."

This is a statement we (Brad and Warren) both might make—with stress on the word "I"—despite our very significant commitments to Christian faith and life. The complementary statement (without which the first statement is misleading) is, "*We* are Christian." There are countless hidden and unacknowledged "others" that are at work in the story of our Christian lives.

This book is about the truth of these statements, at least as understood within the framework we propose. That is, we are attempting to rethink Christian life within the context of modern theory regarding the nature of the human mind. The theory of *extended cognition* argues that human mental capacities (cognition) are very significantly enhanced ("supersized") by the artifacts, persons, and institutions that we constantly encounter and engage. Just as the hidden women were central to the success of the space program, there are numerous hidden, but nevertheless strongly influential, "others" at work in our Christian lives. Therefore, any description of our intelligence is incomplete without inclusion of factors that are *outside* of our brain and body. Within discussions of extended cognition, one might say, "I am not intelligent, but we are." Here the "we" would include not only other people but also a lot of intelligence-enhancing artifacts that are made available to us through the inventiveness of others. We will attempt to rethink how Christian life might be enhanced—indeed "supersized"—by that which lies outside of our individual selves.[1]

We have both been formed in Christian faith around an implicit (and sometimes explicit) idea that being a Christian was an individual achievement. It was clear that our Christianness (our "spirituality") was contingent on what we were or became within ourselves. What was critical in this view was the current status of an inner, private, individual soul—a status indexed outwardly by manifestations of piety and inwardly by subjective spiritual experiences and feelings. From this point of view, Christianness is primarily about who each of us is as an isolated individual.

Contrary to our early formational histories, we will argue in this book that Christian faith and life exist primarily (but not exclusively) within a network of relationships that serves to enhance Christian life by extending us beyond what we are capable of as independent, private, solo individuals. We believe that *extension* (a word that we will fill up with more significance as we progress) of ourselves into a network of Christian persons and practices serves to "supersize" Christian life well beyond the puny version of this life that we might be able to muster on our own. Thus, in this book we will attempt to paint a picture of Christian life as it might be supersized—that is, made larger, fuller, more effective, and more significantly Christian—as we engage persons, artifacts, and systems outside of ourselves that are within our extended extrapersonal space. Ultimately, we will argue that the idea of extended cognition and the supersizing of Christian life diminishes the distinction between individual and corporate Christianity. We can hardly have one without the other.

---

[1] The term "supersizing" comes from a book by philosopher of mind Andy Clark, *Supersizing the Mind: Embodiment, Action, and Cognitive Extension* (Oxford, UK: Oxford University Press, 2011).

THE GENERAL PLAN OF THIS BOOK

We will develop our case in three sections. In section one, we begin with a short overview of some important issues about human nature, as well as a quick outline of our basic arguments (chapter one). Since we are dealing with information from an unusual domain (philosophy of mind), we thought it would be helpful at the beginning to very roughly outline the entire scope of the argument. To make clear the opposing point of view, we follow this broad sketch with an analysis of what is currently the predominant understanding of Christian life—specifically the emphasis on individual, internal, and private "spirituality" (chapter two).[2]

Section two lays out, in more complete form and finer grain, the theoretical background of our work. First, we review ideas about the embodiment of human nature—that is, the idea that we are bodies, not bodies plus non-physical souls, nor bodies plus immaterial minds (chapter three). This chapter reviews many of the arguments from our previous book, *The Physical Nature of Christian Life*.[3] We then spend two chapters describing the various concepts and implications of extended cognition. Here, we relate ideas about the *extended mind* as they are discussed in modern philosophy of mind, borrowing heavily from philosopher Andy Clark's book *Supersizing the Mind*. We describe the degree to which human minds, even though physical, cannot be considered to be limited to the activity of the brain, or even the brain and body, but are constituted by the coupling of brain, body, and *world*. Mind is not limited to what is in the brain or the brain-body. In chapter four we explain how we as individuals interface with various physical artifacts in ways that enhance our mental capacities beyond our normal human limitations. We then take up the more important idea regarding how intelligence and mind are supersized in the context of human interactions (chapter five). Here the most critical idea is how we join with others in reciprocal extension that supersizes common work. Hopefully all of this will make it clear that human intelligence is manifest most robustly in how we functionally interface with

---

[2]We are particularly speaking of North American evangelical Christian spirituality, although other branches of Christianity may exhibit similar challenges.

[3]Warren S. Brown and Brad D. Strawn, *The Physical Nature of Christian Life: Neuroscience, Psychology, and the Church* (Cambridge, UK: Cambridge University Press, 2012).

and incorporate (that is, plug into) our physical and social environments, rather than how we operate as isolated individuals.

In section three, we attempt to work out the implications of an extended mind within the context of Christian life. We first think about the enhancement of Christian life in the network of relationships that constitute (or should constitute) the church (chapter six). Here we are particularly focused on the emergence of a vital life among the body and the degree to which this constitutes a life that is beyond the scope of an individual Christian. Although we are focused in this book on the "we" of Christian life, life-in-the-we has impact on individuals. Persons are formed as Christians within the context of their nested and extended life within the body. Thus, in chapter seven, we take up the issue of the relationship between individual Christian formation and its connection to churches and congregations. Finally, in chapter eight we turn to sources of extension of Christian life that are beyond the current groups of persons with whom we worship and live as Christians. In chapter eight we consider the sources of the extension of Christian life that are present within Christian traditions, teachings, stories, and practices—that is, extension into the historical accumulation of the wisdom and practices of Christian life.

In chapter nine we take up two questions that we anticipate will occur in the minds of some readers. The first is, Where is this church that fosters extension of parishioners into the life of the church—that is, allows individuals to actively plug into the ecclesia in ways that can supersize Christian life? Another issue that may confuse the reader of this book regards its focus on human nature rather than the nature of God. Since the focus of this book is about human persons and groups (congregations), we emphasize the *immanent* properties of God's work in the lives of Christians as mediated through the earthly body of Christ. With this as our task, we do not speak much about the *transcendent* aspects of God's work in Christian life. We believe God's transcendent activity (unmediated and wholly-other) to be an important part of the grand story, but not the part of the story we deal with in this book. Our focus will be the ways individuals may socially and ecclesiastically transcend their isolated "selves" within the ongoing, immanent activity of God through his people. A powerful way of enlarging (supersizing)

Christian life is through God's immanent activity within human relationships—most notably in the life of the church.

Finally, chapter ten concludes the book with three conceptual metaphors that illustrate and contextualize the general nature of the new paradigm of Christian life and the church that we have been discussing. We talk about the extension of mind in navigating a large ship, hidden cognitive extensions that were a part of the US space project, and Paul's metaphor of the church as a body in his letter to the Romans.

TO WHOM WE ARE WRITING AND WHY IT MATTERS

Pastors. For pastors (who we understand as practical theologians working away in the trenches of everyday life and ministry), the ideas expressed in this book will be helpful in reconceptualizing the life of the church in ways that avoid some of the traps of the overprofessionalization of ministry. It is tempting to understand church in a hierarchical framework where professional clergy are responsible for all of the vision casting, planning, and implementation of ministry. Laypersons become infected with this view, coming to understand church as a preplanned, programmatic endeavor, rather than an interactive community where life and ministry spring up from within the body. Hopefully, this book will give new language and perspective with which to conceptualize church life and pastoral leadership.

Students training for various ministries. Our hopes and concerns for pastors also translate to perspectives we believe are helpful to students training for ministry (parish or parachurch, including adjunctive ministries such as faith-based mental health professions). It is the hope that the ideas we present will inspire imaginations about how to develop a vital community of life and faith.

Seminaries often attempt to instill correct theological thinking (Christian orthodoxy) in their students. While this is important, orthopraxy (i.e., right living) is equally important. Seminarians often don't feel nearly as well trained on issues of orthopraxy as they do on orthodoxy. A robust orthopraxy should integrate practical theology with the best of what we currently know of the nature of persons (physically, cognitively, and socially). This book will open up a few topics in the current understanding of human nature and put them in conversation with practical theology and the life of the local church.

Invested laypersons. It is our hope that laypersons who read this book will come to understand that the *church* is not the clergy, the denomination, or specific rites and practices, or even the doctrine, but is a group of followers of Christ who understand themselves as embodied, engaged, enacting, and extending into one another's lives for the sake of the world and the glory of God. It matters *how* you are connected into the body of Christ not just for your own Christian life but also for the sake of the life of the entire body. Our Christian lives are made more robust and supersized as we connect into the interdependent web of congregants that constitutes the local church. If we stand aside in our "spiritual" individuality, we will be lured into the trap of transferring the cultural narratives of consumerism, executive management, and entertainment into the story of our lives. An individualist approach to Christian life and the church results in what is not a genuine body of Christ but rather a nonchurch—that is, "a loose association of independently spiritual persons."[4]

POINTS OF CLARITY

It is important to be clear about two points before we start. First, what do we mean when we use the term *church*? This will become clearer as you read through the book, but we can hint at it here. We *don't* necessarily mean a building, formal polity, committees, or even articles of faith (although all of these have a place). What we *do* mean is a local body of believers that gather regularly for worship, formation, and service. But to be a church, the local group must become interactively entangled in such a way that extension happens (we will say much more about this as we go along). There are practices of the Christian faith that, when done in ways that foster an extended faith, bring about a fuller and more robust Christian life. Even if a church is not formally constituted (denomination, building, explicit polity, or stated doctrine), it would most likely include historical practices of the church, a life based in Scripture, and both an inward and outward focus of service. Finally, as we understand it, the church is always local, particular, and contextualized. Again, the church as we describe it is not created by the intelligence and

---

[4]Brown and Strawn, *The Physical Nature of Christian Life*, 139.

willpower of humans working together like a social club. We acknowledge the power of the Holy Spirit to work through natural processes (which we attempt to describe) to make the church the church.

A second point to clarify is that, as we talk in this book about the supersizing benefits of extension and interactive "soft coupling," there is an implicit notion that these processes necessarily result in what is more beneficial, life enhancing, and Christian. However, we must caution our readers (as we often caution ourselves) that it is possible to interactively extend into, and have supersized, that which calls itself Christian, but is ultimately harmful, life limiting, lacking in Christian virtue, and/or theologically heretical. We can all imagine churches (or perhaps have experienced churches) where what gets supersized is less than the best of Christian life.

Finally, our hope and prayer is that you, our readers, will gain a richer imagination of Christian life that does not settle easily for puny individualist options, but rather sees the possibility of Christian life being supersized by what is beyond you as an individual and accessible in a body of believers—that is, in the life of the church. Part of this richer imagination involves an appreciation of the hidden figures in our Christian lives.

Section One

THE NATURE OF THE PERSON

As indicated in our prologue, we are concerned about the truth of the statement, "*We* are Christian." This statement entails a move away from an understanding of Christian faith and life as individual achievements, and a move toward realization of the degree to which both faith and life are constituted and enlarged by extension of ourselves into the corporate life of the body of Christ that makes up a local congregation.

In chapter one we sketch the broad outlines of the nature of our arguments, particularly the ideas from the theory of extended cognition that seed our review of the nature of Christian life. We describe our concern regarding the consequences of the predominant view of persons as constituted by two parts, a body and a soul, privileging of the soul and disregarding or discrediting of the body. This view plays a critical role in seeding the current understanding of spirituality as inward and private. To this end, we describe briefly the alternative idea that persons are embodied (bodies, not bodies plus souls); are embedded within physical, social, and cultural environments; and extend their mental processes to include the tools or other persons that are being engaged at the moment. This view also argues that humans are adept at incorporating what is outside of their brains and bodies in order to enhance (supersize) mental processes.

The ideas of embodied and extended cognition raise questions about the nature of spirituality and Christianity—do these lie within ourselves as individuals, or do they exist (partly or entirely) within interpersonal and congregational spaces? Chapter two describes current models of spirituality within this framework, while considering an alternative view of the role of the corporate church body. For some, church and worship are understood primarily as ways to enrich inner subjective experiences of faith. For others, community is considered critical because the embodied nature of persons means that faith must be learned and lived. What we offer to this latter group is a perspective and a vocabulary for conceptualizing the importance of interactivity in the church body as both constituting and enhancing Christian life.

Chapter
1

MINDING CHRISTIAN LIFE

BETHANY'S STORY

Toward the end of the service, I hesitated before approaching the Eucharist table. I was in the midst of writing a college paper on the Eucharist, meth addiction, and the church. I asked myself: Where is this faithful church I'm supposed to be writing about and if it exists, will my meth addicted brother ever be a part of it? Why isn't my brother any better? Will he ever be? And even if he were here sitting beside me, how the hell does partaking in the Eucharist change anything? I was quite certain that I had been entertaining foolish hopes that would never be realized. But I thought of the words spoken to Jesus: "Lord, I believe. Help my unbelief!" In that same spirit, I approached the Eucharist table and prayed, "God, I go in doubt, but I go."

Jan and Warren were serving the Eucharist that day. Jan was probably the first person to speak with me when I came to the church for the first time last year. Within the first month or two of being in the church, my sister-in-law, Destiny, had been diagnosed with cancer and my brother, Josh, had relapsed. Jan remembered their names, frequently asked how they were doing, and told me she was praying for them. Months had passed and my sister-in-law's cancer had left, but my brother's addiction remained. Jan still asked about my brother most Sundays.

I first approached Warren to take the bread. "The body of Christ, broken for you," he said. I proceeded to dip the bread into the cup of juice in Jan's hands.

"The blood of Christ, shed for you," she whispered.

"Thanks be to God," I replied.

". . . and for Josh and his family," she continued.

The blood of Christ, shed for you—and for Josh and his family. I was struck. While Jan frequently asked about my brother and had served me the Eucharist on other occasions, she had never said those words while serving me, and I had never approached the Eucharist table thinking more about my brother. For the first time in months, I let myself hope again. Jan's words gave me the courage to believe that my brother was not forgotten, that he was not alone, that maybe he would live and not die, and that maybe his life wouldn't feel so much like death.

The next day, I had coffee with our pastor. When I asked him his thoughts on the connection between the Eucharist, church, and addiction, he said: "I don't think there's anything magical about it . . . lot of times you don't believe this stuff, but you're doing this with a body and they believe for you. An individualistic spirituality is not going to get an addict far, it seems to me. But a communal spirituality is able to hear 'I don't believe this crap,' and yet respond, 'I know, but I do, and I believe this for you.'"

He later said, "And that's what Jan did. She believed for you when you didn't." In this liturgy, people believe for one another in the midst of profound doubt and become corporately what they had not been as individuals—a knitted body witnessing to the love of Christ that gathers with all of us addicts. This gathering occurs in the depths of suffering and in the proclamation of hope.[1]

If there is a single, simple, pithy message in this book it is this: No one is Christian (or "spiritual") entirely on their own. Rather, it is the body of Christ (your church, hopefully) that establishes, nourishes, and enhances Christian life. This life (involving faith, hope, and love) is not our own but is what comes to exist first within the life of the body, then eventually within us. A life cannot be robustly Christian lived entirely on one's own. However, when this life is extended into a body of believers, our puny individual Christian life becomes "supersized"—broader, deeper, richer, and more robust than it could ever be on its own.

Bethany was in the grip of doubt, made more salient by her attempts to write a paper involving her brother and the sacrament of Eucharist. The faith and hope that she could not hold on her own was held for her by her church,

---

[1] This story by Bethany Grigsby is adapted with permission from her contribution to *Mountainside Perennial: Memory for the Sake of Hope*, a publication of Mountainside Communion in Monrovia, California.

and made clear to her by Jan's ministry in Eucharist that particular day. Attached to the body, Bethany was able to be part of a corporate faith that was beyond her individual capacity. She was able to have faith and hope because she was worshiping and experiencing Christian life within a body that allowed her to extend into a shared pool of faith and hope.

This extension of Christian life out of our inner individual selves and into the external world of congregational life is what we explore in this book. If we ignore the more embodied and extended life of ecclesial community, we are at risk of constructing for ourselves a Christian life that is isolated, private, hidden within, and dependent on our feelings. This is problematic in that it unknowingly "Christianizes" the dominant Western narratives of individualism and consumerism. The church becomes a marketplace individuals attend to obtain goods (spiritual good feelings) that they then take with them into their week to survive the "world." Clergy become the information experts that deliver these "goods," and parishioners are the "consumers" who acquire them. In this model, the others with whom I worship are of no particular importance, other than perhaps sharing the costs of the production—in which case watching church at home on a screen may be as meaningful as attending. While it has been noted that Sunday morning in America is one of the most segregated hours of the week,[2] it may also be one of the loneliest. This is very different from the image in the New Testament of a small house church that meets for meals, worship, life together, and service in the neighborhood. If Christian life is not about individuals, but rather about a body of people, what might this mean for our understanding of the life of churches and congregations?

UNDERSTANDING CHRISTIAN SPIRITUALITY

We begin with a confession. We are not big fans of the term *spirituality*, at least not as it is typically used and understood. Despite some degree of lip service to church and Christian community, "spirituality" in the North American evangelical context is usually presumed to be something about

---

[2]This was an oft-quoted phrase by Martin Luther King Jr.; see, for example, Paul Edwards' blog, "Sunday at 11: 'The most segregated hour in this nation,'" October 9, 2010, www.godandculture.com/blog/sunday-at-11-the-most-segregated-hour-in-this-nation.

individual persons. It is understood as a quality of one's personal relationship with God. Even though there are things we often point to as outer evidences (litmus tests) of a person's spirituality (as in a "tree [that] bears good fruit," Matthew 7:16-18 ESV), these outer things we presume to be imperfect reflections of something that is, in reality, inward and private. What is more, many of the sermons we hear, books we read, or Christian conferences we attend convince us that greater spirituality is something that we achieve (or receive) on our own, as individuals who are distinct from other Christians. The church may help me in some way, but my spirituality is mine.

This view of spirituality shares much in common with our individualistic views of the nature of sin, morality, and virtue. These attributes are certainly more outward and behavioral, typically involving the quality of our interactions with other people. Nevertheless, they are understood as expressions of the inner qualities of individual persons. They are outward manifestations of inward and private resources. Again, while circumstances may play some role, my sin, morality, spirituality, and virtue are entirely mine.

This ubiquitous Christian individualism rests heavily on our belief that the essence of being human is that we have a soul (or self)[3]—a part of us that is private, inside, and entirely unique to us. This inner something is the "real me." It is also considered the locus and bedrock of spirituality. We relate to God only because of, and through, our inner soul that is also our "true self." We generally assume that everything that is really important about ourselves and others is hidden inside as features of the self or soul. However, as we have argued elsewhere[4] (and will develop further in the following chapters), this idea of a private individual soul is not inherently Christian and is, in the end, not helpful in our understanding of Christian life and the nature of the church.[5]

We argued in our previous book for a more embodied understanding of the nature of persons, and for recognizing the embeddedness of our selves

---

[3]We recognize that in some traditions and especially in academic parlance there are differences between concepts such as soul, spirit, and self. In the North American evangelical context of average laypersons that we are primarily concerned with, we find that these terms are not well defined and subsequently are used interchangeably.

[4]Warren S. Brown and Brad D. Strawn, *The Physical Nature of Christian Life: Neuroscience, Psychology, and the Church* (Cambridge, UK: Cambridge University Press, 2012).

[5]While commitment to body-soul dualism is a critical source of this sort of inwardness and individualism, it is reinforced by other trends. It is also a product of post-Kantian subjectivity and the various "solas" of the Protestant Reformation with its intentional detachment from historic Christian tradition as a genuine authority for Christian life.

(bodies) within family, social, cultural, and ecclesial contexts. We are inherently bodies entangled in the worlds we occupy. Thus, words like *mind, soul, spirit, self,* and *person* point to the same whole, embodied individual, but with particular attention to different *aspects* of us as whole persons.[6] In their recent book, Jeeves and Ludwig write extensively about the degree to which spirituality needs to be understood as both embodied and situationally embedded.[7] We wish, in this book, to further this argument by considering the degree to which we should consider the mind (and thus the person) to *extend*, at various times and in various ways, out beyond our individual bodies to encompass currently available aspects of the external world of persons and things. Our primary goal is to consider what the implications of notions about the extension of the self might have for understanding Christian life.

For us, then, *spirituality* (if and when we use this word) is the gradual and relational process of being transformed into the image and likeness of Jesus as persons and as groups resulting from experiences of extended (and thus supersized) corporate Christian life.[8] It is about an embodied life understood as embedded in a world infiltrated by the Spirit of God—a Christian life which is enhanced by extension of the person into interactions with a local body of Christ.

Thus, we happily interchange the word *spirituality* with our preferred term *Christian life.* Such life is not individual, private, or inward, nor is it correlated with an emotional state. The formation of Christian life is a gradual process that takes place over time in the context of a larger body of Christian persons. This life is not one that we possess but one in which we outwardly participate. And it is important to continually view this corporate life as having an outward telos or goal—it is not primarily about individual believers, nor even about particular churches or congregations, but about the reign of God in the world.

---

[6]As anthropological monists, or better, holists, we use terms such as these to describe aspects of the whole person not reified separate parts or internal agents, or special religious sensors that are needed for God to communicate with humans.
[7]Malcolm A. Jeeves and Thomas E. Ludwig, *Psychological Science and Christian Faith: Insights and Enrichments from Constructive Dialogue* (West Conshohocken, PA: Templeton Foundation Press, 2018), 136-44.
[8]We are discussing a natural process that falls under the category of natural theology.

MINDS AND PERSONS

In addition to our Wesleyan theological tradition, our understanding of Christian life is also strongly shaped by our understanding of the nature of persons and the human mind. Rather than keep these domains of thought compartmentalized, we strive to integrate the growing understanding of the nature of persons into a resonant field of coherent understanding with practical theology.[9] That is, in an attempt to understand what it means to be human and to be Christian, we have tried to bring into conversation Scripture, the historical understandings of the church (i.e., tradition), human understanding (i.e., experience), new scientific discoveries (empirical method), and current philosophical arguments (i.e., reason).[10]

Ideas about the nature of the human mind have shifted significantly in recent decades. The shift is toward understanding mind (and thus persons) as more deeply encompassing the entire body (embodied cognition), as well as the surrounding situation with which a person is interacting (our embeddedness, or situatedness). This shift in ideas about the mind has been motivated by a revised view of how the brain brings about mind. For most of the last half of the twentieth century, the mind (understood to be the brain) was presumed to be very much like a computer. Computers are given highly abstract information (that is, data are input) to be worked on (computations) based on abstract instructions about what to do with the information (a computer program). Once the computations are complete, the computer outputs some form of abstract information which we interpret as rational conclusions. This is referred to as "information processing," and human minds have been thought to be information processors—we assimilate abstract data, do computations, arrive at abstract conclusions, and then find ways to use these abstractions to guide action. In this view of mind, some of these abstract computational processes are experienced as conscious thought.

However, despite some very rough similarities, the brain (and also the mind) is *not* a computer—it is different in very fundamental ways. The difference (or

---

[9]Warren S. Brown, "Resonance: A Model for Relating Science, Psychology, and Faith," *Journal of Psychology and Christianity* 23 (2004): 110-20.

[10]This four-fold way of discovering truth based on tradition, experience, reason, and Scripture has been called the Wesleyan Quadrilateral. We break reason into two categories: reason that includes philosophy and logic and reason that is the outcome of the scientific enterprise.

at least one major difference) is the contrast between *abstract* and *embodied*. To illustrate this difference, the word "shout," as a written word, is abstract, but the meaning of this word (i.e., a loud vocal act) to a person hearing or reading the word is not a mental abstraction but body-knowledge. We know "shouting" because we know what it is to do it (a motor act of our body) or hear it (a sensory experience). What is critical is that what our brains know is rooted in memories of bodily acts and sensory experiences. It does not know "shout" in the form of a computer-like abstraction. What we know is grounded in what we can remember doing or sensing.

Of course, human thought gets a lot more complicated than this, but the complications do not entirely escape their sensory and motor embodiment. One way things can become mentally more complex takes advantage of our ability to metaphorically stretch physically embodied knowledge to cover more abstract (less immediately physical) notions. We might say that a headline "shouts," but this metaphoric reference is understood by its link to our history of bodily experiences. As another example, the phenomenon of time is abstract—it does not have an immediate sensorimotor thing that it designates. So, we think about time using experiences that are linked to the passage of time—as in the experienced duration of movement (time "passes," "goes by," "speeds up," "slows down"), or as a quantity that gets progressively used up like sand in an hourglass (time is "spent," "runs out," "elapses," "disappears").[11] Thus, the embodied view of mind argues that thinking does not need abstractions when it can store and manipulate sensorimotor memories. Representations that we might want to call "abstract" probably exist in the mind, but most of what we know remains, or has deep roots in, body-knowledge.

We have previously argued that Christian life can be better understood by viewing minds and persons as embodied.[12] If our bodies are deeply implicated in the processes we call "mind," then to be Christian is not to have acquired certain abstract information, or to believe specific abstract propositions. Rather, it is constituted by particular sorts of bodily, interactive, social, and narrative knowledge that we use in thinking and deciding how to interact

---

[11]George Lakoff and Mark Johnson, *Philosophy in the Flesh: The Embodied Mind and Its Challenge to Western Thought* (New York: Basic, 1999), 137-69.
[12]Brown and Strawn, *The Physical Nature of Christian Life.*

with this situation or that person. We will elaborate this understanding of the human mind throughout this book in order to help us reshape our understanding of Christian life—particularly how human relationships (that is, embodied persons interacting with other embodied persons) are so essential to Christian life.

THE EXTENSION OF MIND

The force that specifically motivates the writing of this book is our encounter with a deeper understanding of the human mind called *extended cognition*.[13] In this view, mind and its capacities include not just the brain and what happens inside it, or even the brain and body, but mind also must include those aspects of the physical and social world with which a person is currently actively engaged. In most situations our mental processes (and thus our intelligence) include what is going on in the interactions *between* us and the physical or social environment. A very simple example is trying to remember a name. I can interact with my smartphone contacts list (physical environment), or I might ask someone else (social environment). In either case, my mental process of remembering includes, for a brief moment, my interactions with the world outside my body—my mind becomes an extended process that includes more than just me. My individually faulty memory has been *supersized* by what is available beyond my brain and body. Typically, the thinking we do is not simply something that goes on inside us but a process that incorporates what occurs outside of us as we interact with the physical and social environment. Thought is a dynamic process of engagement with the world— a process in which the world does not play a passive role. Interactive engagement with the environment significantly enhances mental capacities.

The idea that what constitutes our mind will often include things outside our brain and body is not at all intuitive. Our habits of thought and language cause us to presume that mind is an entirely internal process that *uses* (but does not include) the body or elements of the world. The idea of an extended mind suggests that the body and the world become interactively coupled with the activity of the brain in dynamic loops where the processing boundaries

---

[13] Andy Clark, *Supersizing the Mind: Embodiment, Action, and Cognitive Extension* (Oxford, UK: Oxford University Press, 2011).

between brain, body, and world become blurred or nonexistent. So much of the technology we use is transparent with respect to its impact on our subjective experience of thinking and problem solving. The net outcome of our capacity to incorporate resources of body and world is to markedly enhance our mental capacities—to supersize our minds.

SUPERSIZING CHRISTIAN LIFE

We are intrigued by the idea of the extension of mind with respect to its implications for understanding Christian life, revisiting ideas of spirituality, and taking more seriously the life of a church. If it is true that mind is supersized by extension—that is, by interactions with physical and social surroundings—might this also apply to our Christian lives and what we refer to as our "spirituality"?

Thus, a goal of this book is to explore the idea of the enhancement of Christian life through processes of extension. Can individual Christian life be supersized—made larger, deeper, and more robust—by extension into corporate Christian life? For example, can belief be understood to extend beyond our individual minds and into the community of faith? This would mean that we don't believe all by ourselves, but we believe with others in the church. The body of Christ holds and upholds our belief, just like we saw with Bethany in the opening story. In times when we are incapable of believing on our own, belief nevertheless can be operative because we experience it within the extended and supersized life of the body of Christ—the church. However, the contributions of the body are often hidden from our view (much like the "hidden figures" in the development of space capsules). In this book we will try to bring into focus how individuals connect to the larger whole, rather than how the whole (the church) serves the individual.

To this context, Paul's idea that the church is to be the "body of Christ" can be taken quite literally. At least in North America[14] the focus in most evangelical Christian thought has been on the individual life of the believer. The individual has held dominance over the collective.[15] When individualism

---

[14]In different parts of the world and different cultures one can find evidence of a much more collectivist ecclesial and spiritual Christianity. While our concern is a predominantly Western evangelical Christianity, we believe that this branch of the church has much to learn from other cultures.

[15]We also recognize that even in the West, and especially in younger generations, there is an encouraging move toward a more communal ecclesiology. We hope that this book will continue to provide evidence and support for this work.

takes precedent in Christian life, the "spirituality" of separate persons is seen as the goal and focus. However, Scripture seems to reverse that order, placing focus first on the collective—the people, the church, the body. In 1 Corinthians 12:12-31 Paul helps us see that the end goal is not the individual but the whole, the body, the church. Individuals are important and significant as they come to serve an important role to the larger whole. Paul's metaphor of the body is so powerful because, just as an eye makes no sense (has no life-giving function) apart from the body, an individual Christian life makes no sense apart from the body of Christ. We cannot detach ourselves from one another. We cannot survive without one another. If one suffers, all suffer. And we certainly cannot engage in the Great Commission that Christ has given us without one another!

CHURCH AS SUPERSIZING CHRISTIAN LIFE

With these ideas in mind, an important goal of this book is to reconsider the life of the church in the context of the possibility for the enhancement of Christian life by extension. We will argue that the extended nature of mind provides a critical rationale for why the interactively corporate modes of the church are so powerful and transformative—for example, prayers, liturgies, singing, and teaching, as well as corporate expressions of service, compassionate care for one another, and even social gatherings.

If we consider Christian life and faith within an information processing model where the understanding of, and assent to, abstract ideas is most important, then anything involving the body or other persons is of only marginal importance, and the primary goal of church would be to reform the content of the abstract information held within the privacy of the minds of individual persons. Get the right information inside the individual person and the right behavior will come out. Or, if we consider spirituality to exist primarily in subjective experiences (mystical or emotional) that are internal and private, then the goal of church is to enhance the frequency and intensity of such subjective experiences. However, if the core of Christian life involves extended interactions with a worshiping body of believers (outward, not inward), then new and important light is shed on all those contexts in which "two or three are gathered" in the name of Christ (Matthew 18:20 ESV). We are not attempting to eliminate individual practices or disciplines that have been in the church universal for centuries (some of which are quite embodied and communal). Rather, we are attempting to reimagine them in light of embodied and extended cognition, and in so doing encourage a re-understanding of these disciplines without the individualism which characterizes much of evangelicalism.

What might it mean for the church to focus less on the promotion of individual "spirituality" (of whatever kind), and rather recognize the fact that in congregations we can take part in a corporate life that can supersize the otherwise puny Christian faith and life of which we are individually capable? How should we not only understand church but actually go about *doing* church in such a way as to avoid promoting disembodied and disconnected (individualistic) spirituality? What would result from viewing Christian faith and life as extended—that is, as existing primarily *between* Christian persons? How can a church engage in embodied practices that supersize and extend Christian life? What are the implications of this view for worship practices, preaching, relational interactions, and service opportunities? And, like Bethany from the opening story, how can we foster belief that is enhanced as it is extended into a faith that is held and nurtured by a community?

MODERN SPIRITUALITY

"I'M SPIRITUAL, NOT RELIGIOUS." This is a commonly heard phrase in today's post-Christian age. It is often meant to differentiate something worthwhile (spirituality) from something considered problematic and dispensable (religion). While persons who employ this phrase are usually quite clear about what is bad about religion (e.g., it's authoritarian, legalistic, intolerant, shaming, etc.), they are often hard-pressed to clearly articulate what they mean by spirituality and why it is better (other than it is not religion!). But short of a clear understanding of spirituality, the statement begs the question: Is spirituality something that transcends religion, or is it inextricably entangled with religion such that it can only be articulated when anchored in religious life and practice? Can one speak of a free-floating spirituality, or must it be tied to religious life, such that one must speak of Buddhist spirituality, or Jewish spirituality, or Catholic spirituality? Rodney Clapp argues that "one reason the term [spirituality] is so popular is that *by itself* it is vague, amorphous. Or, to put it positively, it is an elastic and capacious word—it can contain multitudes. . . . Consequently, against conventional grammar, *spirituality* appears to be a noun decisively determined by its adjective."[1]

In this book, we are not particularly interested in such generic, amorphous spirituality. Instead, we are interested in *Christian* spirituality and, even more so, Christian life. We prefer to speak of "Christian life" rather than "spirituality" in an attempt to avoid problematic dualities (e.g., soul and body, spirituality and religiousness, sacred and secular, experience and action, inner and outer) that are often implicit in discussions of spirituality and spiritual formation.

---

[1]Rodney Clapp, *Tortured Wonders: Christian Spirituality for People, Not Angels* (Grand Rapids: Brazos Press, 2004), 13.

This chapter is concerned with the contemporary North American evangelical lay understanding of spirituality, spiritual formation, and the nature of Christian life. In looking at this topic, we face an issue that has a long history but is particularly evident in modern movements in spiritual formation and spiritual disciplines and practices—a problem that is entangled with modernity, evangelical ecclesiology, and theological anthropology. We are concerned that when we misunderstand the nature of persons, we misconstrue Christian spirituality and the nature of Christian life. What we presume about persons affects how we understand the term *spirituality* and has significant implications for how we practice our faith.

In the previous chapter, we began to define and discuss the nature of spirituality as it is currently understood, and as we understand it. We particularly lamented (but without developing the ideas extensively) that the predominant understanding of evangelical spirituality in North America is something that is inward, individual, and private. In this chapter, we attempt to characterize and critique more clearly the current notion of spirituality.

HISTORICAL ROOTS OF MODERN IDEAS OF SPIRITUALITY

Before considering modern views of spirituality, it is helpful to remind ourselves of the philosophical-historical background that has shaped the modern perspective. The roots of what is currently the predominant view of spirituality can be found in body-soul dualism—the view that humans are constituted by two parts, a physical body and a nonphysical soul. This idea originated in the philosophy of Plato, which differentiated nonmaterial forms (that which is really real) from the material world (a mere shadow of the real). Thus, the nonmaterial part of the person (soul) came to be more valued and privileged compared to the material body. This perspective had a strong influence on Western Christian thought, primarily through the writings of St. Augustine (although there are other lines of influence, such as the Gnostics of early Christianity).

For our purposes, it is important to focus on what has been described as the "turn inward" found in Augustine's philosophy of human nature and spiritual life.[2] In the context of a Platonic dualism, Augustine imagined that

---

[2]Phillip Cary, *Augustine's Invention of the Inner Self: The Legacy of a Christian Platonist* (Oxford, UK: Oxford University Press, 2000).

the soul dwelt inside persons.[3] Thus, greater spirituality came about by the cultivation of the inner soul, which consequently became the primary focus of Christian faith. Owen Thomas—emeritus professor of theology at the Episcopal Divinity School in Cambridge, Massachusetts, and past president of the American Theological Society—in his book *Christian Life and Practice: Anglican Essays*, thoughtfully critiques the modern spirituality movement which he believes has come to dominate the church since the 1970s.[4] Thomas describes Augustine's view in the following way, "The Platonic distinctions of 'spirit/matter, higher/lower, eternal/temporal, immutable/changing is described by Augustine, not just occasionally and peripherally, but centrally and essentially in terms of inner/outer.' And the reason is that the inner is the road to God." As Thomas quotes Augustine, "Do not go outward; return within yourself. In the inward person dwells the truth."[5]

The ideas of Augustine became a core part of the understanding of human nature and human spirituality within the Christian church. For example, the turn inward fostered by the writings of Augustine can be explicitly seen a millennium later in the mysticism and inner life advocated in the lives and teachings of Teresa of Avila and St. John of the Cross. The body-soul (outer versus inner) distinction was also central to the analytic philosophy of human nature proposed by René Descartes, which perpetuated the views of Augustine within philosophy.[6]

Rodney Clapp also recounts this history in his book *Tortured Wonders: Christian Spirituality for People, Not Angels*. Clapp writes that the original disembodiment of Christian spirituality was rooted in the early writings of the church fathers and mothers, who often spoke of the body as a burden. Clapp argues that their distrust of the body was related to human mortality, which makes sense in a time and place where death was a constant threat. Mortality and the fear of sexual passions created a distrust of the fragility of the body and engendered a Christian spirituality that despised the body. To

---

[3]To be historically accurate, Augustine was likely more influenced by Neoplatonists like Plotinus than Plato.
[4]While we are writing primarily about the evangelical church in North America, it is interesting to find an Anglican equally concerned.
[5]Owen C. Thomas, "Interiority and Christian Spirituality," *Journal of Religion* 80, no. 1 (2000): 45.
[6]We cover the history of the origins of Christian dualism in chapter two of our previous book, Warren S. Brown and Brad D. Strawn, *The Physical Nature of Christian Life: Neuroscience, Psychology, and the Church* (Cambridge, UK: Cambridge University Press, 2012).

protect the *real* person from the transience and suffering of life, the body was seen as little more than a container or a machine.[7] For Augustine, the inner is where one finds the true self and God, while the outer is problematic because it is mortal, fallen, and material. In essence, the inner and outer are exact opposites with the inner being where the real person resides—at the center of all that is most important.

One important point we wish to emphasize in this broad-brush account of the origins of body-soul dualism, and the accompanying distinction between inner and outer in modern spirituality, is that the origins of these ideas are not found in the Bible. While we have for centuries read biblical passages within this Augustinian framework, it is essentially foreign to the texts themselves.[8] This realization has caused a great many theologians and biblical scholars to abandon such dualism, seeing in Scripture a more holistic and embodied view of persons.

INNER SPIRITUALITY

In the *Dictionary of Christian Spirituality*, editor Glen Scorgie defines spirituality in the following way:

> Spirituality in its generic sense is about connecting with the transcendent and being changed by it. It involves an *encounter* with the transcendent (or the numinous, the Real, or whatever is ultimately important) and then the beneficial *effects* of that encounter on a person or a community. It is about establishing a transforming connection to something more—a connection that will shape who we become and how we will live.[9]

Scorgie points out that there are two distinct Christian versions of this definition. The narrow version he describes as "concerned with experiencing the presence, voice, and consolations of God in a direct, right-here-right-now way."[10] This understanding of spirituality puts heavy emphasis on inner subjective experience as an index of the spiritual state of the inner soul.

---

[7] Clapp, *Tortured Wonders*, 29-32.
[8] Joel B. Green, *Body, Soul, and Human Life: The Nature of Humanity in the Bible* (Grand Rapids: Brazos Press, 2008).
[9] Glen Scorgie, "Overview of Christian Spirituality," in *Dictionary of Christian Spirituality*, ed. Glen Scorgie (Grand Rapids: Zondervan, 2011), 27; emphasis in original.
[10] Scorgie, "Overview of Christian Spirituality," 27.

According to Scorgie, a more holistic version, while affirming the possibility of directly experiencing God, has "insisted that there is more to being a Christian than this. Holistic spirituality is about living *all of life* before God. . . . It also includes things like repentance, moral renewal, soul crafting, community building, witness, service, and faithfulness to one's calling."[11] This view shifts the understanding of spirituality outward toward the nature of Christian life.

The narrow inner version described by Scorgie has gained prominence in a large portion of modern evangelical Christianity. The inner here-and-now version has had great influence on popular notions of spirituality and spiritual formation. It is presumed that internal changes in the believer's heart bring about secondary changes in outward behavior. In fact, outward behavior becomes a kind of litmus test of true inward spirituality—not the real thing, just an indicator.

A useful case study of what Scorgie is referring to as the narrow inner view may be found in the Renovaré movement. Renovaré is originally linked to the work of writer Richard Foster and provides resources and conferences directed at enhancing Christian spirituality. An example of the predominance of an inward, direct, and experiential understanding of spirituality can be seen in the definition of spiritual formation given on the Renovaré website:

> We are all spiritual beings. We have physical bodies, but our lives are largely driven by an unseen part of us. There is an immaterial center in us that shapes the way we see the world and ourselves, directs the choices we make, and guides our actions. *Our spirit is the most important part of who we are.* And yet we rarely spend time developing our inner life. That's what Spiritual Formation is all about.[12]

Modern North American evangelical spirituality resonates with this definition from Renovaré. This understanding of spirituality is consistent with what Scorgie describes as "narrow." That is, practices and disciplines (e.g., worship, prayer, spiritual meditation) are designed to engender inner events— "communion with God," "encountering Jesus," "receiving a word," "having a

---

[11] Scorgie, "Overview of Christian Spirituality," 27-28; emphasis in original.
[12] "Spiritual Formation," Renovaré, https://renovare.org/about/ideas/spiritual-formation, emphasis added.

personal relationship with Jesus"—in other words, inner, here-and-now *experiences*. Ultimately, the value of these experiences, and what they mean with respect to spiritual thriving, is assessed by how one *feels*. While we suspect that these writers would argue that this inward work should lead to outward fruit, the outward work seems merely a litmus test that indicates the inner holiness of the person.

This tendency to measure one's spiritual status via feelings is behind statements such as, "I just don't feel close to God," or "My spiritual life is just dry right now." Because this understanding of spirituality is about things inside, it privileges the inner over the outer, the soul over the body, feelings over behavior, and the individual over the community. Besides being a truncated understanding of spirituality, this approach of assessing spiritual status via felt experience may lead to believers becoming disillusioned and discouraged in their spiritual journeys when they don't feel what they believe they are supposed to feel—for example, when they are sick, depressed, stressed, or grieving.

Our aim is not to suggest that the narrow form of spirituality that Scorgie posits is entirely misguided in its *goal* of formation. However, we are concerned that this narrow understanding of spirituality is thin and inadequate, and that a more embodied view of Christian spirituality engenders a more robust and vital Christian life. The overemphasis on the internal and individualistic spirituality found in a vast number of evangelical churches in North America cripples Christian faith because it distracts us from enacted, shared, and communal faith.

There are two pathways that have branched from the Augustinian understanding of spirituality as inward and private: (a) a disconnection of spirituality from the embodied, everyday life of Christian persons, and (b) a loss of the view of spirituality as embedded in communal life. While these two outcomes are entangled, the first problem is essentially related to views of ourselves, and the second is related to views of the church. In what follows, we take on each of these two issues. These problems are the outgrowth of a kind of "folk theology of spirituality" that has developed primarily in evangelical churches in the West who read this literature through the lens of contemporary individualism characteristic of much of American Christianity.

DISEMBODIED SPIRITUAL LIFE

The idea that an Augustinian understanding of persons might lead to problematic understandings of spirituality has been taken up by Anglican professor and writer Owen Thomas. Thomas characterizes much of the literature on spirituality as disembodied, with its "pervasive emphasis and focus . . . on the inner or interior life as distinct from the outer, bodily, and communal life."[13] As an example of such inwardness, he quotes revered spiritual writer Thomas Merton who wrote in a letter to his friends shortly before his death, "Our real journey is interior; it is a matter of growth, deepening, and an ever greater surrender to the creative action of love and grace in our hearts."[14] Owen Thomas sees this inner/outer distinction at the heart of the problem mentioned at the beginning of the chapter—the conflict presumed by many between spirituality and religion, "whereas religion deals with the outer life, that is, institutions, traditions, practices, doctrines, and moral codes, spirituality treats the *inner* life, which thus tends to be *individualized* and *privatized*."[15] He argues that if spirituality is conceptualized primarily as an issue of the interior life, it is "mistaken philosophically, theologically, and ethically and that it needs to be redressed not only to a more balanced view of the inner/outer relation but also to an emphasis on the outer as primary and as a major source of the inner."[16]

Fergus Kerr writes, in his book *Theology After Wittgenstein*, about the degree to which the inner/outer distinction can affect even one's understanding of prayer.

> Spiritual writers in the last three centuries or so have driven many devout people into believing that the only real prayer is silent, wordless, "private." . . . It is amazing how often devout people think that liturgical worship is not really prayer unless they have been injecting special "meaning" to make the words work. The inclination is to say that participation consists in private goings-on inside the head. . . . There is . . . a central strain in modern Christian piety which puts all the emphasis on people's secret thoughts and hidden sins.[17]

[13]Thomas, "Interiority and Christian Spirituality," 41.
[14]As cited in Thomas, "Interiority and Christian Spirituality," 41.
[15]Thomas, "Interiority and Christian Spirituality," 42, emphasis added.
[16]Thomas, "Interiority and Christian Spirituality," 42.
[17]Fergus Kerr, *Theology After Wittgenstein*, 2nd ed. (Oxford, UK: Basil Blackwell, 1997), 172-173. For Wittgenstein even the meanings of the words in spoken prayers are communal in that they are established in local language interactions and usage.

Here we see clearly how an Augustinian anthropology lends itself to a disembodied spirituality. This understanding of spirituality privileges the inner soul (or spirit) over the outer body and dramatically impacts how one understands Christian practices and even the goal of Christian life. This kind of disembodied spirituality is what Rodney Clapp calls "modern spirituality" as opposed to Christian spirituality.[18]

MODERN SPIRITUALITY AND THE CASE OF RENOVARÉ

The hierarchical prioritizing of the inner (the "soul") over the outer (the "body") that springs from a dualist framework is pervasive in the modern literature on spirituality. Despite what these authors mean or intend, their writing is often misunderstood by evangelical readers. Perhaps one of the clearest examples of this (although obviously not the only example) is Renovaré, a movement that was founded by Richard Foster and deeply influenced by the writings of Christian philosopher Dallas Willard. We quoted earlier a definition of spirituality from the Renovaré website which emphasized an inner, disembodied spirituality. Listen also to Dallas Willard from his celebrated text *Renovation of the Heart: Putting on the Character of Christ.*

> Spiritual transformation into Christlikeness, I have said, is the process of forming the *inner* world of the human self in such a way that it takes on the character of the *inner* being of Jesus himself. The result is that the *"outer"* life of the individual increasingly becomes a natural expression of the *inner* reality of Jesus and of his teachings. Doing what he said and did increasingly becomes a part of who we are.[19]

From this statement, it would be easy to conclude that the inner is primary and superior to the outer, because inside is where the real person exists. If change is to happen it must happen from the inside out.

The writings of Renovaré have undoubtedly ministered to millions as they have argued persuasively for the practices of spiritual disciplines and their role in the process of sanctification. Writers such as Foster and Willard

---

[18]Clapp, *Tortured Wonders*, 15.
[19]Dallas Willard, *Renovation of the Heart: Putting on the Character of Christ* (Colorado Springs: NavPress, 2002), Kindle loc. 3159, emphasis added.

acknowledge how spiritual practices are clearly embodied, and they recognize the importance of the body in the process of sanctification (that is, behavioral change). Dallas Willard seems to espouse a tripartite theological anthropology (that is, humans are made up of three things: body, soul, and spirit). His biographer, Gary Moon, suggests that Willard was not a pure dualist or trichotomist but a "both/and plus" thinker.[20] Nevertheless, his anthropology could be read as hierarchical, privileging the inner experiences of the spirit and soul over the outer life of the body. From this viewpoint, the body is important as a means to an end, remaining separate and distinct from the soul (or spirit), which is presumed to be the primary focus of spiritual life.

Willard's writing regarding the body can be confusing, perhaps due to his attempt to be a "both/and" anthropologist. He seems to both extol the importance of the body for the spiritual life, and at times to blame it for most of our religious problems (i.e., sin). In chapter nine of *Renovation of the Heart*, we find an example of this confusing approach.

> For good or evil, *the body lies right at the center of the spiritual life*—a strange combination of words to most people. One can immediately see all around us that the human body is a (perhaps in some case even *the*) primary barrier to conformity to Christ. But this certainly was not God's intent for the body. It is not in the nature of the body as such. (The body is not inherently evil.) Nor is it even *caused* by the body. But still it is a fact that the body usually hinders people in doing what they know to be good and right. Being formed in evil it, in turn, fosters evil and constantly runs ahead of our good intentions—but in the opposite direction.[21]

In the same chapter (titled "Transforming the Body"), Willard states that the body is a good thing, that God made it for good, and that this is why the way of Jesus is incarnational. Then he states, "For most people, on the other hand, their body governs their life. And that is the problem."[22] It is not difficult to hear in his writings the kind of inner/outer distinction that Owen Thomas warns against. In this framework, we have a good soul and a bad, or

---

[20]Gary Moon, personal communication, 2017.
[21]Willard, *Renovation of the Heart*, Kindle loc. 3172, italics in the original.
[22]Willard, *Renovation of the Heart*, Kindle loc. 3171.

at least highly problematic, body (although not originally bad). And this body is not only separate but also inferior to the "real spiritual person"—the inner soul or spirit.

After doing some exegetical work on Romans 5–8 where Paul speaks at length about the body, Willard writes:

> The GREATEST DANGER to our prospects for spiritual transformation at this point is that we will fail to take all this talk about our bodily parts very literally. It may help us to consider ordinary situations of temptation. We said earlier that temptation is a matter of being inclined to do what is wrong. But where do these inclinations primarily reside? The answer is, they primarily exist in the parts of our body.[23]

Like Willard, most evangelical Christians read passages like those in Romans from the standpoint of a biblical interpretation rooted in an Augustinian body-soul dualism—a theological anthropology not supported by contemporary biblical interpretations, and difficult to integrate with a modern understanding of the mind.

DISEMBODIED AND DISCONNECTED FROM COMMUNITY

Perhaps what is most misleading to the average evangelical Christian layperson reading many contemporary writers on spirituality is how the presumption of dualism (or tripartism), and consequent understanding of spirituality as inward, may lead to the conclusion, *I am not my body. My body is something that I have, and it is a problem. It is not part of my thinking, my being, my learning, my rationality, my emotions, or my spirituality. The body is something to be mastered, conquered, and disciplined into compliance, but it is not me.* In this view, the "real me" or the "true self" is inside, private, and individual. Inside is where all the important stuff really happens. The body is just a carrier—and a highly problematic one at that. Therefore, we use our mind/soul/spirit (whatever we believe to be inside) to train the body so that it behaves. The body is an inconvenient necessity, but "not me."

The second problematic issue related to the inwardness fostered by a dualistic and disembodied Augustinian view is that it may lean toward a form of

---

[23]Willard, *Renovation of the Heart*, Kindle loc. 3316, caps in the original.

Christian life that is not deeply embedded in and engaged with communal life.[24] A dualistic and disembodied spirituality leads to the idea that the *real* and most important part of me is inward, individual, and private. Consequently, spirituality becomes equated with the state of the soul. Therefore, spirituality is only secondarily related to outward bodily actions, and has little if anything to do with interactions with the bodies of other people.

As evidence of this view of spirituality, consider the growing number of people who are "spiritual but not religious" and the massive decline in church attendance in North America. Consider also the implications of the ideas expressed in the lines of some contemporary worship songs: "All I need is You, Lord," or "I want only for you." While this is only a small sample, such expressions of solitary Christian experience (e.g., "just Jesus and me") are widespread in contemporary Christian worship songs. Of course, we can also find expressions that sound similar in Wesleyan and Methodist hymns (such as "Jesus, Lover of My Soul"), and even in the Psalter there are individualistic psalms as well as communal psalms of lament (Psalm 44) and thanksgiving (Psalm 67). The social contexts in which these individualistic psalms and hymns were composed and sung were very different in terms of the relationship between individuals and their community. The Israelites knew that they had been called and set apart as a people. Even their individualistic psalms would have been used in corporate worship. Early Methodism was also organized around intensely social, communal, and behavioral groups and practices. So while the language of the Israelites and Methodists could, at times, be individual, both were set in highly communal contexts.

We have no doubt that we *need* Jesus, but it's the "all" that is easily misunderstood. Jesus is best found within a body of believers ("where two or three are gathered together," Matthew 18:20 KJV), or among those in most need. Jesus' first words to his disciples were not "Come *experience* me," rather, they were "Follow me" (Matthew 4:19)—that is, a call to a particular embodied, embedded, and enacted way of life.

Disembodied spirituality, with its inner/outer distinction, is not simply a problem of the disconnection of the body from spirituality, but is also

---

[24]Brown and Strawn, *The Physical Nature of Christian Life*, chaps. 7-8.

problematic with respect to the disconnection of our Christian lives from the lives of others. This individualistic tendency has implications for our understanding of the Bible. As Owen Thomas writes, "It appears, for example, in the tendency to interpret *entos* in Luke 17:21 ('The kingdom of God is among you') as 'within' rather than 'among,' whereas the overwhelming majority of exegetes agree that it means 'among.'"[25]

Because concepts that seem to refer to a disembodied inner life are frequently used in Christian language (and songs), it is important to be clear about what we mean by them. Influenced by Wittgenstein, Thomas suggests that "the inner/outer distinction is essentially a linguistic construction"[26]— that is, a spatial metaphor for something that is not really spatial at all. For Thomas, inner is a metaphor that only makes sense if it is understood as dependent on the outer. Inner is the felt sense and experience of the actions of life.[27] Thomas argues that Christian life, as understood through the biblical witness of Scripture, must give primacy to how one lives one's actual life in the body (the outer), rather than inner experiences.

The position that inner is a metaphorical expression that points to the felt experiences of the actions of the body has three important implications for Thomas's view of Christianity. First, it implies a renewed interest and emphasis on the body, which means that "more attention should be paid to responsibility for the outer world of the body and the community, including the material, economic, social, political, and historical world rather than an exclusive focus on the soul or interior life in Christian spirituality."[28] Second, there needs to be a shift from the inner world of a person as central in Christian spirituality to the reign of God as central. This would reverse the emphasis on spirituality as primarily private, inward, and individual. Finally, this view implies a new emphasis on practice in Christian formation. However, this practice cannot be the kind that is understood as simply a means of nourishment for the private, inward life of the solitary believer which then bubbles out in good works, passing the litmus test of the indicator of true inner spirituality.

---

[25]Thomas, "Interiority and Christian Spirituality," 52, italics in the original.

[26]Thomas, "Interiority and Christian Spirituality," 56.

[27]For a description of thought as action-simulation, see Andy Clark, *Being There: Putting Brain, Body, and World Together Again* (Cambridge, MA: MIT Press, 1997).

[28]Thomas, "Interiority and Christian Spirituality," 58.

Treating embodied life as primary and prior suggests that formation in the Christian life should focus on the practices of the outer life, such as public worship, the building up of the community, the service of those in need, and participation in the struggle for justice and peace, rather than on the disciplines of the inner life, such as silence, meditation, and contemplation. It is not that these latter disciplines should be excluded but that they should be considered as rooted in communal and public practice.

Thomas's views are squarely within the domain that Scorgie refers to as a holistic view of Christian spirituality, including, but not limited to, moral renewal, community building, service, and faithfulness to one's calling.[29] Thankfully there has been an increase in contemporary Christian writers who embrace the body—to honor it, to think deeply on its implications for spiritual life, and even to better incorporate it into theology.[30] While the approach we will suggest here differs in some significant ways from these writers, these developments point toward an increase in Christian thinkers recognizing the centrality of the human body.

CHALLENGING INWARD SPIRITUALITY

The implications of a more embodied understanding of spirituality are particularly telling for our understanding of the church and corporate Christian life. Rodney Clapp argues that "Christian spirituality" (as opposed to "modern spirituality") is about bodies socially embedded in particular times and places. Clapp points out that this view is suggested by the Lord's Prayer in which *we* pray (as a gathering of physical creatures) for "daily bread," and for God's will to be done "this day," and in which we are reminded that we face temptations in community.[31] For Clapp, the church is central for spiritual formation. "Christian spirituality is the whole person's participation and formation in the church—Christ's body, the Spirit's public—which exists to entice and call the world back to its Creator, its true purpose, and its only real hope."[32]

---

[29]Scorgie, "Overview of Christian Spirituality," 28.
[30]Tara M. Owens, *Embracing the Body: Finding God in Our Flesh and Bones* (Downers Grove, IL: InterVarsity Press, 2015); Stephanie Paulsell, *Honoring the Body: Meditations on a Christian Practice* (San Francisco: Jossey-Bass, 2002); Rob Moll, *What Your Body Knows About God: How We Are Designed to Connect, Serve, and Thrive* (Downers Grove, IL: InterVarsity Press, 2014); Luke Timothy Johnson, *The Revelatory Body: Theology as Inductive Art* (Grand Rapids: Eerdmans, 2015).
[31]Clapp, *Tortured Wonders*, 23-24.
[32]Clapp, *Tortured Wonders*, 18.

While Clapp conceptualizes the origin of the problem a bit differently than Thomas, their conclusions are remarkably similar. For Clapp, inwardness and individuality are interlinked. He believes that the core problem lies in the modern West's emphasis on the individual body (person) as central and the social body as a derivative. An example of this individual-first problem can be found in William James's *Varieties of Religious Experience,* in which he argues that an individual person first has a spiritual experience, and then chooses to associate with others who have had a similar experience.[33] Clapp argues that this is not how premodern individuals, or St. Paul, would have understood persons and community.

This individual focus is also a critical problem in the modern understanding of spirituality since it ignores the root of religious/spiritual experiences in prior communal life. Clapp writes,

> Christianity sinks its roots into the reality and priority of the social or corporate body. In such a vision, the identity and welfare of each member are embedded in and intertwined with the identity and welfare of the whole, the many united. Without an appreciation of the social body, orthodox Christianity can simply make no sense.[34]

He points out that it is impossible for a Christian to flourish apart from Christian community, in the same way that many professionals (such as artists) cannot flourish apart from their professional guilds. While he is not disparaging of individual, daily spiritual exercises, "they do not precede corporate worship. They are derived from corporate worship and circle back to find their fulfillment in corporate worship. . . . Ultimately, if others do not pray with me, Christian faith and spirituality will become small and trivial, beaten down by a world so much bigger and more interesting than my individual obsessions and desires."[35]

CONTRASTING VIEWS OF CHRISTIAN LIFE

In this chapter we have argued that the modern view of spirituality is confusing, and even potentially misleading, in arguing, on the one hand, that the

---

[33]William James, *Varieties of Religious Experience: A Study in Human Nature* (New York: The Modern Library, 1902).
[34]Clapp, *Tortured Wonders,* 73.
[35]Clapp, *Tortured Wonders,* 88-89.

body is good, and on the other hand, that it is the source of our troubles. This ambiguity about the body is rooted in the dualism of the inner/outer split between a spiritual inner self and a body that often acts sinfully. Consistent with this view, many who are interested in spirituality but not religiousness (both Christian and non-Christian) want an inward and individual spirituality apart from tradition, community, institutions, or organized religions—that is, a spirituality that doesn't implicate the body, and isn't inextricably embedded within networks of other bodies. As we will describe in the next section of this book, this view of persons is at odds with current philosophical and theological anthropology, including what is known about the nature of the mind from advances in psychological science and neuropsychology.

For writers like Thomas and Clapp, Christian spirituality is fully embodied and inextricably embedded within community. However, in their reaction to inwardness and individualism there is a lack of clarity regarding *why* Christian faith and life is best understood as rooted in congregations and communities. That is, we find a significant gap in these arguments with respect to what it is about human functioning that is more robust when persons are linked into networks of other persons. In section two we attempt to answer the *why* question regarding individuals in communities.

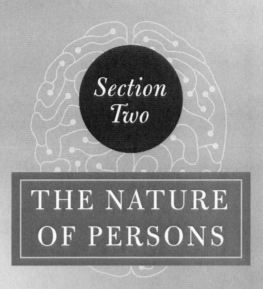

Section Two

THE NATURE OF PERSONS

W HY IS CHRISTIAN LIFE MORE ROBUST when persons are linked into networks of other Christians? In section two we attempt to answer this question by providing what we believe to be a clearer view of human nature. The view comes largely from work in the philosophy of mind, particularly regarding the embodied, embedded, and extended nature of human mind and intelligence.

Thus, chapter three (on the embodiment of personhood) describes the basic arguments for the physical nature of human minds. We are particularly concerned with making it clear that such a view does not eliminate nor short-circuit a rich understanding of Christian faith and life. In fact, it is our view that an embodied understanding of persons puts Christian life and practice on a firmer foundation.

Even though the mind is physical, we argue in chapter four (on the physical extension of mind) and chapter five (on the social extension of mind) that it cannot be considered to be limited to the activity of the brain, or even the brain and body. Rather, the mind is constituted by the interactive coupling of brain, body, and world. In chapter four we concentrate on how the human mind is enhanced by the interface of brain and body with various extrabody physical artifacts and tools. Chapter five elaborates on the notions of interfacing with, and incorporation of, artifacts outside the body, by a discussion of how intelligence and mind are supersized in the context of interpersonal interactions. The net message coming out of arguments regarding the extended nature of mind is that human intelligence is constituted and enhanced by how we functionally interface with and incorporate aspects of our physical and social environments, rather than intelligence being the outcome of how smart we are when operating entirely on our own. Although of some relevance here, we leave discussions of extension into the wider reaches of accumulated knowledge and culture for chapter eight.

Chapter
3

MINDING BODIES

IN THE PREVIOUS CHAPTER we reviewed the primary themes of recent teaching on spiritual formation, as well as some of the critiques of this understanding of spirituality. The primary critique centered around the focus on inward states of the soul/spirit/self.[1] As a consequence, outward, bodily, enacted Christian life is understood as a secondary manifestation of a more important reality of an inward state. The outward life of a Christian was important only insofar as it reflected a mature and vibrant inner life.[2]

In our previous book, *The Physical Nature of Christian Life*, we described how the source of this view of spirituality is nested in body-soul dualism—the idea that persons are a combination of two distinct parts, a body and a soul. This has been the dominant view of human nature in Western culture and in the church since the time of St. Augustine. What follows in this chapter is a review and expansion of the alternative to dualism—that is, the embodiment of human nature. Our intention in this chapter is to anchor our arguments in an understanding of persons as physically *embodied* and situationally *embedded*, rather than as selves or souls enclosed within bodies. With these ideas in mind, the following two chapters venture into the main theme of this book—the thesis that humans are *extended* beings that are able to include within their current mental functioning and Christian lives objects and persons outside of their own bodies.

---

[1]Once again, we recognize that different writers use these terms differently, but we use them interchangeably to recognize the need for different ways to describe aspects of very complex whole human persons.

[2]Some material in chapters three through five is adapted from Warren S. Brown, "Knowing Ourselves as Embodied, Embedded and Relationally Extended," *Zygon* 52, no. 3 (2017): 864-79. DOI: 10.1111/zygo.12349.

BODY-SOUL DUALISM

Body-soul dualism asserts that humans are composites of two different parts, a material body and a nonmaterial "mind" or "soul" (these two terms are not distinguished in early philosophical writings and function similarly within the context of this discussion). Within most forms of dualism, the soul/mind is considered (at least implicitly) to be superior to the body and must rule over it. Thus, the soul/mind is understood as the source of all that is distinctly and importantly human—rationality, sociality, spirituality, personal identity, etc. In addition, only the soul is immortal, while the body is mortal and subject to decay.[3]

Medieval philosopher René Descartes provided what was perhaps the most radical assertion of a distinction between the body and the mind/soul. Since Descartes could not imagine that rational thought was something that could be done by a body—by physiological processes—he argued that thinking could not be a material process. Thus, rationality had to be substantially different and distinct from the functions of the body and its actions in the world. Thinking had to be a nonmaterial, disembodied process. Thus, for Descartes, thinking was accomplished by a nonmaterial soul/mind which was hidden, private, and available only through introspection. The actions of the body were accomplished in a secondary manner by the rational, nonmaterial mind interacting with the irrational, material body.

The views of Descartes were based on the work of St. Augustine many centuries earlier. The impact of Augustine has been described as the "turn inward."[4] Augustine followed the ancient Greek philosopher Plato, for whom physical objects (like the body) were mere shadows of ideal forms. Thus the real person cannot be the physical body but must be a nonmaterial form. For Augustine, this nonmaterial reality of the person was an inner soul/mind. Thus, to know oneself was to turn inward in introspection. That is, as Augustine described it, thinking amounts to exploration of the inner, nonmaterial world of the mind/soul. From Augustine's teaching arose the modern understanding of spiritual life and spiritual disciplines as made up of inward events and subjective states, as we reviewed in the previous chapters.

---

[3]Body-soul dualism has been well described and critiqued by Nancey Murphy in her introduction and chapter appearing in Warren S. Brown, Nancey Murphy, and Newton Malony, eds., *Whatever Happened to the Soul? Scientific and Theological Portraits of Human Nature* (Minneapolis: Fortress Press, 1998), 1-29, 127-48.

[4]Phillip Cary, *Augustine's Invention of the Inner Self: The Legacy of a Christian Platonist* (Oxford, UK: Oxford University Press, 2000).

Dualism is difficult to maintain in the light of modern neuroscience in that most human experiences and capacities have been shown to emerge from identifiable patterns of brain activity. Capacities such as rational thought, emotional experience, interpersonal relationality, moral deliberation, and even religious experiences arise out of brain processes that have mostly already been identified and at least roughly described.[5] Although there are scientific differences of opinion and theory about the details of the brain processes involved in these higher cognitive capacities, there is little doubt about the physical embodiment of mental phenomena (most starkly illustrated by their absence or deficiency with certain forms of brain damage). Even the so-called "hard problem" of subjective consciousness[6] has been assailed by good neurobiological theory.[7] In light of this, a nonmaterial soul/mind does not seem to account for much.[8] This does not mean, however, that persons can be reduced to molecules and atoms. It is not meant to imply that humans are simply determined creatures that have no free will. We will discuss this below, but for now our point is that to be Christian and to understand human uniqueness does not require positing something immaterial and immortal *within* the person. What makes humans unique is much more about how God *chooses to interact* with humans who are a part of his physical creation.

We have argued elsewhere that dualism is also problematic for reasons of its impact on our understanding of human life and the practical theology of Christian life. If this inner soul is superior to the body and rules over it, and if it is the soul that is eternal, then each person must focus on caring for and nurturing their own soul, first and foremost. Consequently, one's body and outward behavior are secondary priorities. The primary task of the church,

[5]This point discussed in Malcolm A. Jeeves and Warren S. Brown, *Neuroscience, Psychology, and Religion: Illusions, Delusions, and Realities about Human Nature* (West Conshohocken, PA: Templeton Foundation Press, 2009). With respect to the neuroscience of religious experiences see Warren S. Brown, "The Brain, Religion, and Baseball: Comments on the Potential for a Neurology of Religion" in *Where God and Science Meet: How Brain and Evolutionary Studies Alter Our Understanding of Religion; Volume II: The Neurology of Religious Experience,* ed. Patrick McNamara (Westport, CT: Praeger Publishers, 2006), 229-44. While it appears that the full complement of human cognitive capacities is neurobiologically embodied, they are nevertheless, in their full manifestation, emergent nonreducible properties of the entire brain/body/world. Their emergent complexity often demands mentalistic language that need not signal mind/body dualism.
[6]David Chalmers, "Facing Up to the Problem of Consciousness," *Journal of Consciousness Studies* 2, no. 3 (1995): 200-219.
[7]Antonio Damasio, *The Feeling of What Happens: Body and Emotion in the Making of Consciousness* (New York: Harcourt, 1999); Gerald Edelman and Giulio Tononi, *Consciousness: How Matter Becomes Imagination* (London: Allen Lane, 2000).
[8]The argument that the idea of a nonmaterial soul/mind does not seem to account for much does not make such dualism incoherent, just a seemingly unnecessary construct.

then, becomes fostering inner change (salvation of souls), and only if time and energy permit should attention be paid to the physical, economic, and social well-being of other persons.⁹

Despite near universal rejection of mind/body dualism in modern philosophy of mind, cognitive science, and neuroscience, the implications of the Augustinian/Cartesian view of human nature persists in neuroscience, which has been characterized as Cartesian by philosopher Daniel Dennett.¹⁰ Dennett argues that most scientists would now agree that thinking is a property of neural processes. However, the brain is understood as a processor of abstract information that is functionally separate from the rest of the body. Thus, the *mind-body* dualism of the Augustinian/Cartesian view has been replaced by *brain-body* dualism—that is, Cartesian materialism. In this view, the body interacts with the inner brain through sensory inputs and motor outputs that require encoding of information into abstract neural representations—like sequences of bits in a digital computer. In effect, the brain is viewed as a neural computer to which a body has been attached, much like we attach peripherals like keyboards and printers to digital computers. This understanding of mind is known as the *information processing model* and has been predominant in cognitive psychology and neuroscience for the last fifty years.¹¹ Clearly, it is difficult to escape from centuries of Western thought that has ignored the body in favor of an inner reality (whether a soul or a brain) that is the *real* person.

Thus, to know one's self in the Cartesian worldview (whether the earlier Augustinian/Cartesian world of body-mind dualism, or the more modern world of Cartesian materialism) is to attend to what is going on in the private, inner recesses of the soul/mind or brain by introspection. What is to be known about ourselves in the conceptual world of Descartes and Augustine is the nature of a ghostly, ephemeral, nonmaterial inner being. In the world

⁹Warren S. Brown and Brad D. Strawn, *The Physical Nature of Christian Life: Neuroscience, Psychology, and the Church* (Cambridge, UK: Cambridge University Press, 2012). See also Warren S. Brown, Sarah D. Marion, and Brad D. Strawn, "Human Relationality, Spiritual Formation, and Wesleyan Communities" in *Wesleyan Theology and Social Science: The Dance of Practical Divinity and Discovery*, eds. M. Kathryn Armistead, Brad D. Strawn, and Ronald W. Wright (Cambridge, UK: Cambridge University Press, 2010), 95-112.
¹⁰Daniel C. Dennett, *Consciousness Explained* (Little, NY: Brown & Co., 1991).
¹¹George A. Miller, "The Cognitive Revolution: A Historical Perspective," *Trends in Cognitive Sciences* 7, no. 3 (2003): 141-44.

of Cartesian materialism, one must know something about the current state of a neural computational cloud. In both cases, these inner constructs are only distantly connected to one's body and behavior or to the outer world that one inhabits.

PHYSICALISM, EMBODIMENT, AND EMBEDDEDNESS

Our primary focus in this book is not so much to critique the Cartesian view (that work has been done elsewhere[12]), but beginning with its presumed difficulties, we intend to explore a more embodied alternative that is faithful to Christian theology. If dualism is not tenable, is the only other option a kind of reductionistic materialism where humans are nothing but molecules and atoms, with no free will and no moral agency? Thankfully in psychology, philosophy, and theology there are a number of alternatives to dualism that seem to capture the fundamental nature of personhood but that also have the advantage of being more resonant with cognitive science and neuropsychology. These models are given a variety of labels in philosophical debates, such as nonreductive physicalism, emergent monism, dual-aspect monism, emergent holistic dualism, etc. In these alternative perspectives, the concept of the emergence of human capacities from patterns of neurobiological activity plays a central role. Generally, these views assert the fundamental physical nature of humankind (i.e., embodiment) but with a strong qualifier that the mental functioning of persons cannot be reduced to "nothing but" physiology. Although we are physical bodies running on physiological processes, there emerges from these processes a genuine and efficacious mental life that we experience as thinking, deciding, remembering, and feeling. In the more technical language of philosophy of mind, we would say that the hypercomplex physical system that is a human being has aspects of the whole person (like thinking, deciding, and feeling) that are emergent from the ongoing interplay of the parts (cells, neurons, neural systems, the brain, etc.) but cannot be said

---

[12]Joel B. Green, *Body, Soul, and Human Life: The Nature of Humanity in the Bible* (Grand Rapids: Baker Academic, 2008); Alicia Juarrero, *Dynamics in Action: Intentional Behavior as a Complex System* (Cambridge, MA: MIT Press, 1999); Jeeves and Brown, *Neuroscience, Psychology and Religion*; Nancey Murphy, *Bodies and Souls, or Spirited Bodies?* (Cambridge, UK: Cambridge Press, 2006); Nancey Murphy and Warren S. Brown, *Did My Neurons Make Me Do It? Philosophical and Neurobiological Perspectives on Moral Responsibility and Free Will* (Oxford, UK: Oxford University Press, 2007).

to be properties of the parts themselves.[13] So, the point is that there are re-sources within theories of embodiment that are consistent with the idea of persons being thoughtful and responsible agents. Thus, it is not necessary to assume that these capacities are the manifestation of a nonmaterial soul/mind. Nor is it necessary to presume that these properties are nothing more than the determinative outcome of the cellular processes of neurobiology.

However, exactly what emerges in the cognitive operations of the hyper-complex physical system of a human being is conditioned by the physical, social, and cultural environment in which it is embedded. Particularly during human development, mind forms its capacities, gains knowledge of the world, and organizes itself through interactions with the world it occupies. One reason this process of environmental influence is particularly powerful in hu-mankind is that the human cerebral cortex (the outer, wrinkled shell where most higher-order mental processes take place) is slower to develop than that of other primates. Slow physical development of the brain allows for a longer period of openness in the development of its knowledge and capacities for effectively interacting with the environment. Thus, while genetics certainly play a general role in mental development, most of the patterns of functional connectivity within the brain that emerge as "mind" come about in direct response to environmental challenges and interactions. We are formed by the characteristics of our physical and social embeddedness.[14] Balswick, King, and Reimer describe a similar developmental understanding in their work, *The Reciprocating Self.* They conceptualize human development as a recip-rocating process between person and environment, and further delve into what this means for humans who are made in the image of God.[15]

The best explanation of how higher-order properties (like mind) emerge in a hypercomplex system (like the human brain and body) in response to environmental challenges can be found in the theory and research on complex

---

[13]Murphy, *Bodies and Souls, or Spirited Bodies?*; Murphy and Brown, *Did My Neurons Make Me Do It?* See also Green, *Body, Soul, and Human Life*; Joel B. Green, ed., *What About the Soul? Neuroscience and Christian Anthropology* (Nashville: Abing-don Press, 2004); and Jeeves and Brown, *Neuroscience, Psychology, and Religion.*

[14]Steven Quartz and Terrence J. Sejnowski, *Liars, Lovers, and Heroes: What the New Brain Science Reveals About How We Become Who We Are* (New York: William Morrow, 2003).

[15]Jack O. Balswick, Pamela Ebstyne King, and Kevin S. Reimer, *The Reciprocating Self: Human Development in Theological Perspective*, 2nd ed. (Downers Grove, IL: InterVarsity Press, 2016).

dynamic systems.[16] Although somewhat technical, the theory of dynamic systems provides a reasonable explanation of how new knowledge and capacities emerge as this very complex system that is the brain organizes its patterns of neural interactivity in order to improve the person's capacities to meet new environmental challenges (physical, social, or cultural). When the very complex biological system that is "me" faces a new adaptive challenge, the elements within me must reorganize their patterns of interactivity to express behaviors that meet the new challenge—which is what we call "learning." Thus, if the brain/body is a complex dynamic system (as many believe[17]), then the properties and capacities of mind are formed throughout life as the person faces new adaptive challenges and is forced to reorganize to meet the challenges. The impact of continual processes of reorganization is particularly salient in the development of the "mind" of children but is also an ongoing process in adulthood.

BODY AS THE ROOT OF MIND

Neuroscience makes it increasingly clear that mental activity is a functional outcome of the physiological activity of the brain. This is one meaning of the idea of "embodied"—that is, that the soul/mind is not a nonmaterial part (as it is in dualism) but is an outcome of the physical process of the brain. However, as we have seen, this restricted concept of embodiment is consistent with Cartesian materialism—we merely consider "soul" or "mind" to be exclusively embodied within the brain, and we end up with brain-body dualism.

However, the idea of *embodied cognition* goes further than the mere assertion of the physicality of mind. Embodied cognition argues that the processes of thinking actually involve the entire body—that is, what we refer to as our "mind" is grounded in interactions between the brain and the body, and is not solely dependent on brain processes.[18] Because cognition is about action, the basic constituents of thought and mind emerge from rapid interactive brain-body loops—decisions made in the brain about immediate action,

---

[16]Juarrero, *Dynamics in Action.*

[17]Juarrero, *Dynamics in Action*; Murphy and Brown, *Did My Neurons Make Me Do It?*

[18]Andy Clark, *Being There: Putting Brain, Body, and World Together Again* (Cambridge, MA: MIT Press, 1997); and John A. Teske, "From Embodied to Extended Cognition," *Zygon* 48 (2013): 759-87.

then bodily activity, then sensory feedback regarding the outcome of action, then adjustments for further action, and on and on. For example, the mental process of multiplying two three-digit numbers (something that is very difficult if not impossible to do just in your head) involves constant loops of action-feedback-next action (typically involving paper and pencil)—that is, multiplying each digit of the second number by the first digit of the first number, while writing down the results as you go, including indicating any values carried, and then proceeding to multiplying the second number by the second digit of the first, and so forth. Each small step serves to cue the next step based on the feedback from the ongoing calculation. Mind (or "minding") is our ongoing action-feedback engagement with the situation with which we must interact at the moment. Mind is constituted by action loops.[19]

The relationship between the body and mind, and the organization of the content of mind from life experiences, have implications for the nature of particular minds—why one person's mind might be different from another's. If persons have different bodily experiences, they would have differently constituted minds. Consider this—if you had the *body* of an elephant but the same physical *brain* that you have, you would have a very different *mind*, because your mind would have been built from your bodily experiences of interacting with the world. If you had an elephant's body, you would have built your mind through very different ways of interacting with the world—for example, using a trunk rather than hands to manipulate things and learn about the properties of objects. So, to the degree that one person's bodily experiences have been different from another person's, their minds would be different.[20]

This idea of the relationship between body and mind can also be understood by imagining the life of an individual born without hands or arms. Such a person would encounter the world differently, for example, manipulating objects with their feet rather than hands. Thus, the person's experience of these objects would be somewhat different. Some objects might be experienced only by seeing, since they are objects that persons with a typical body

---

[19]The idea of mind as a processing loop is explored in detail by Douglas Hofstadter, *I Am a Strange Loop* (New York: Basic Books, 2007). Also see Murphy and Brown, *Did My Neurons Make Me Do It?*; and Jeeves and Brown, *Neuroscience, Psychology, and Religion: Illusions, Delusions, and Realities About Human Nature*.

[20]This is also an interesting way to think about differences in cultures. Persons in different cultures experience and interact in different ways with different environments, both physical and social.

could handle with hands but that could not be explored and manipulated with feet. In some areas (not all, of course), this person would have a mind constructed from different sorts of experiences and interactions with the world than a person with hands and arms—not necessarily better or worse, but certainly different.

Christian Keysers, in studying the phenomena associated with mirror neurons, describes the brain events associated with viewing pictures of the manual activities of other individuals.[21] When viewing a picture of a person drinking from a cup, the arm and hand area of the motor cortex becomes active in persons with typical body morphology. This suggests that we understand pictures of actions by using our own motor systems to implicitly go through the same actions. However, in a person born without arms, who uses their feet to manipulate objects, the foot area becomes active when viewing this same picture. That is, when one must drink from a cup using a foot, motor areas of the brain controlling the foot become active when viewing others drinking out of cups, even though the person in the picture is doing so using hands and arms. A person's understanding of cups and drinking are formed by that person's history of embodied interactions with cups and drinking— for example, manual or pedal.

If we understand the world through bodily interactions, how do we come to understand abstract ideas that have no apparent direct reference to physical things or events—such as "democracy" or "the square root of -1"? A number of philosophers of mind have argued that even abstract concepts that would seem to have no particular embodied representation are understood via metaphorical extensions of bodily experiences associated with action—or at least such ideas begin that way.[22] For example, the concept of "time" is abstract— that is, it does not seem to refer to anything in the physical world with which we can bodily interact. However, we comprehend the abstract idea of time using metaphors based on bodily movement—time passes, slows down or

---

[21]Christian Keysers, *The Empathic Brain: How the Discovery of Mirror Neurons Changes Our Understanding of Human Nature* (self-pub., Amazon Digital Services, 2011), Kindle.
[22]George Lakoff and Mark Johnson, *Philosophy in the Flesh: The Embodied Mind and Its Challenge to Western Thought* (New York: Basic, 1999); Mark L. Johnson, *The Meaning of the Body: Aesthetics of Human Understanding* (Chicago: University of Chicago Press, 2007); George Lakoff and Rafael Nuñez, *Where Mathematics Comes From: How the Embodied Mind Brings Mathematics Into Being* (New York: Basic Books, 2000).

drags, rushes by or flies; events are in the past (we have passed them) or in the future (in front of us). Thus, a metaphorical link to the sensory and motor experiences of movement provides an embodied basis for the semantics of the abstract idea of time.

BODILY REFLECTIVE THINKING

But what about the times when we are thinking but not acting? Isn't this evidence *against* the idea that thinking involves our whole bodies? We obviously have reflective times, like when we are sitting in an easy chair merely thinking about this or that. If it is true that our minds are formed by acting in the world, and thinking is for acting, then action must also be implicated in this reflection—in the seemingly offline, interior, nonactive processes of rumination.

Most theorists who endorse an embodied view of mind consider reflective thinking to be a process of offline sensorimotor *simulation*.[23] We think by imagining (that is, simulating within our motor systems) actions which we might do within various imagined contexts. Even when our bodies are quiet, we think by simulating (imagining) embodied interactions. Simulated acting accomplishes thought, but so also does simulated sensory experience—recalling the visual or auditory or tactile nature of things experienced in the past, as well as re-experiencing the likely bodily feel of imagined actions. When we daydream about our favorite vacation spot and recreational activity, we are reconstituting within our nervous systems remnants of the remembered sensory and motor experiences.[24]

Most importantly, a great deal of what we experience as thought involves the simulation of speech interactions. We simulate conversations with specific others, vague others, or perhaps with ourselves. As you write text of various sorts and are formulating various possible sentences, you may notice that you are imagining yourself actually saying these sentences. Thinking about what to write is simulating things that you might say to your reader. And the process of typing the words is accompanied by an almost audible inner experience of saying the words being typed. Thus, our private thoughts are rehearsals (simulations) of potential actions—things we might say or do in particular circumstances, and

---

[23]Germund Hesslow, "The Current Status of the Simulation Theory of Cognition," *Brain Research* 1428 (2012): 71-79.
[24]We will have more to say about this later when we discuss spiritual disciplines practiced alone.

the likely impact of such saying or doing. Our inner dialogue involves embodied rehearsals of things we might say in imaginary social contexts.

The phenomenon of mirror neurons (described earlier) makes it clear that we can, in fact, run sensorimotor programs in our brains offline, and that it is this sort of simulation that constitutes our understanding of others, ourselves, and the world—particularly the social world.[25] Mirror neurons are neurons (primarily within motor systems of the brain) that respond in the same way while *viewing* the activity of another individual as they do when the observer is *doing* the same motor activity. Thus, understanding the actions of another person appears to require modeling (simulating) the activity being observed within one's own motor control systems. But the activity of the motor systems of the brain involved in such mirroring does not become expressed in bodily actions. We can run simulations of acting offline—i.e., without actually doing the actions. Knowing the meaning and intentions of the behavior of other persons is accomplished by motor simulation in a manner that is similar to our processes of reflective thinking.

EMBODIED MOODS, EMOTIONS, AND EVALUATIONS

The relationship between mind and body also includes the influences of the current state of our bodies on what we experience as our moods, emotions, and evaluations. We utilize the reactions of our bodies to make judgments about the emotional qualities of situations. We judge the emotional state of other persons, or the emotional quality of words and pictures, by implicitly sensing very subtle changes in our own bodies and facial expressions. If something is done to prevent a facial reaction, judgments of emotions become less accurate. For example, it is harder to appreciate (make accurate judgments about) another person's smile if the capacity of our own face to smile is blocked—such as when holding a pencil with our lips in a way that causes our lips to pucker and our brow to furrow. Holding the pencil crossways between the teeth, forcing a smiling expression of our lips, cheeks, and brow, enhances our ability to accurately detect smiles in pictures of faces but makes accurate judgments of frowns more difficult.[26]

---

[25]Keysers, *The Empathic Brain*.
[26]Jamin Halberstadt, Piotr Winkielman, Paula M. Niedenthal, and Nathalie Dalle, "Emotional Conception: How Embodied Emotion Concepts Guide Perception and Facial Action," *Psychological Science* 20, no. 10 (2009): 1254-61, https://doi.org/10.1111/j.1467-9280.2009.02432.x.

Confirmation of the idea that ability to make facial expressions affects one's ability to judge the facial expressions of others comes from studies of women who had received Botox injections for cosmetic treatment of frown lines. This treatment prevents frown-like expressions of the forehead. A side effect of the treatment is a reduced ability to make accurate judgments of subtle emotional expressions in the faces of others. When your face will not make a frown, you can't appreciate the frowns in the faces of others.[27] However, another interesting side effect of Botox treatment of frown lines was reduced levels of depression. When your face no longer easily frowns, you feel less depressed.[28]

It is also true that perceptions and evaluations of our physical context are affected by the state of the body. For example, judgments of the steepness of a hill, or the distance that must be traveled to reach an object seen in the distance, are affected by whether or not one is wearing a heavy backpack, or whether one is particularly tired. The judgment is made not on the basis of the visual information alone, but on the interaction between what we see and how much energy we implicitly estimate it will take us to move our bodies up the hill or toward the distant object.[29]

Finally, memories are so deeply embodied that they interact with our current emotions or body postures. Thus, memories of past events have been shown to be facilitated or inhibited by whether our current emotion is compatible with the memory. In addition, memory is enhanced by adopting a body posture consistent with the posture of our body during the event to be remembered. For example, memory for an event that occurred while jogging is more likely to occur, and likely to be more accurate, while one is currently jogging. Jogging activates jogging memories because our memories are constituted by our bodily experiences.[30]

---

[27]Juan Carlos Baumeister, Guido Papa, and Francesco Foroni, "Deeper than Skin Deep: The Effect of Botulinum Toxin-A on Emotion Processing," *Toxicon* 118 (2016): 86-90, https://doi.org/10.1016/j.toxicon.2016.04.044.

[28]Tillmann H. C. Kruger and M. Axel Wollmer, "Depression—An Emerging Indication for Botulinum Toxin Treatment," *Toxicon* 107 (2015): 154-57, https://doi.org/10.1016/j.toxicon.2015.09.035

[29]Dennis R. Proffitt, "Embodied Perception and the Economy of Action," *Perspectives on Psychological Science* 1, no. 2 (2006): 110-22.

[30]Katinka Dijkstra, Michael P. Kaschak, and Rolf A. Zwaan, "Body Posture Facilitates Retrieval of Autobiographical Memories," *Cognition* 102 (2007): 139-49.

EMBODIED COGNITION AND ARTIFICIAL INTELLIGENCE

The theory of the embodiment of the human mind raises questions about how to understand artificial intelligence (AI)—that is, intelligence embodied in nonbiological systems. How does AI enlighten our understanding of human nature and the embodiment of mind?

The first point to make is that such systems are clearly intelligent—in many cases, remarkably so. It is not a mistake to label these human-created digital artifacts as possessing "intelligence." These systems can do incredibly complex calculations more rapidly and at greater volume than any human being. They can learn (e.g., neural networks). They can detect the meaning of speech and respond appropriately (e.g., Siri and Alexa). They can recognize complex visual images like faces, and can, if mobile, navigate complex environments.

The fact that nonhuman material systems (like computers) can embody such high-level intelligence is an argument for the possibility of the physical embodiment of rationality (a possibility Descartes could not grasp since he did not own a PC). In the case of a computer the physical embodiment is the actual materiality of the computer. In the case of humans, the embodiment is biological (neurophysiological), and the nature of the physical embodiment makes all the difference.

When encountering AI as present in robotic systems, it is easy to be captured by the very impressive outward similarities to humans. Some of the most sophisticated AI systems are embodied in human-looking digital-mechanical robotic bodies (e.g., Honda's ASIMO, NASA's R5 robot, and DARPA's Atlas). Although not in human-like bodies, systems like Siri and Alexa talk to us in very warm and pleasant human voices. In many cases, the AI we encounter seems so very human that we easily impute humanness and a modicum of personhood.

Thus, AI and robotic systems raise inescapable questions about what it means to be human. Is what is embodied in AI or robotic systems *human* intelligence, or intelligence of another kind? While our attention is readily captured by similarities in external appearance and behaviors, it is important to consider the nature of the physical embodiment and what it means for the nature of the intelligence. We have discussed the implications of *embodied* cognition, which argues for the participation of the entire body in human intelligence. The nature of the body influences the nature of the mind (e.g., if you had the same brain but the body of an elephant you would have a very different mind). While we focused on the impact of differences in the outer body, the same argument can be made with respect to differences in internal systems of the body and how these are involved in mental processes.

First of all, if you simply compare even a super computer to the human brain there is a remarkable difference in complexity. The human brain (not to mention the human body) is the most complex thing in the universe. In addition, it is not a digital machine. While some neural phenomena look to be digital (i.e., the information available in the rate of action potentials flowing down the axon of a neuron), there are many forms of very complex analog computations that are complexly enmeshed in the processing networks.

In addition, AI systems are computational information processing systems, as we have described them above. Intelligence in these systems is a product of computations run on abstract codes. Information from the world must be re-represented in digital form in order to be subject to intelligence-manifesting computations on abstractions. In human beings, information re-mains in sensory and motor forms and does not need to be re-represented. Thus, thinking occurs via sensorimotor action simulations that involve the entire body (including the simulation of speech acts). The involvement of the body in thinking can be easily experienced in the autonomic emotional re-sponses that often accompany our thoughts. The body in human mental pro-cessing is not a minimally interconnected set of peripheral devices but is di-rectly involved in the processing. So, the nature of the body constitutes the nature of the mind.

Because emotions are primarily bodily autonomic sensations, it is not pos-sible for a robotic system to have truly human emotions. What stands for "emotions" in AI systems that attempt to take emotions into account is a digital code for a state, perhaps computed from abstract information gleaned in encoded form from the environment, that can be used to compute patterns of reaction—such as seeing a face configured in fear and thus creating an abstract code to represent "fear" but not knowing what it is like physically to be afraid. Because there is not a body with an autonomic system—thus, infor-mation available about such things as heart rate, blood flow (as in blushing), muscle tension, etc.—there cannot be the same sort of feelings in a robot that we understand as our emotions.

Another implication of this difference in the embodiment of cognition is that an AI or robotic system cannot mirror the behavior of other persons in the same way that humans do. Earlier in this chapter we described mirror neurons within the human brain. These are neurons first discovered in the motor system (but also found elsewhere) that respond both when a person moves (acts) and when the person sees another person act in the same way. We understand the actions of others by simulating what it would be like to make the same action with our own bodies. By mirroring the action of the other person in our own brain, we know the feeling of the action, as well as the associated intention. By mirroring actions we also experience the associated affects and emotions. Because a robotic system has a differently constituted body and different internal workings, it cannot truly mirror the actions or feelings of a human person. The consequence of this is an inability for robots to truly experience empathy and participate deeply in interhuman relationships. However, our human tendency to anthropomorphize means we readily *infer* humanness (personhood) in human-like nonhuman systems like robots by mirroring the robot's speech and behavior as if they were produced by our human systems.

THE EMBEDDED BODY

It is important to keep in mind the idea that embodied life always occurs in specific contexts and that contexts condition action. We are always embedded in some ongoing life situation. Thus, the theory of embodied cognition also entails what is known as *situated cognition*.[31] This idea asserts that action, and therefore thinking, does not occur outside of a situation. Mental activity is always about actions embedded within situational contexts—immediately present or imagined. Bodies are always somewhere. Actions always happen in some place at some time. Thus, thinking is always *contextualized* action simulation.

We earlier talked about the embodied simulations that compose our reflections. To sit quietly and consider one of life's situations is to run mental

---

[31]James G. Greeno, "The Situativity of Knowing, Learning, and Research," *American Psychologist* 53, no. 1 (1998): 5-26.

simulations of acting in specific situations and experiencing memories of the sensory consequences of such actions. Such simulation-based thought does not escape its embeddedness in some situations—it cannot occur in a way that is abstracted from specific situations. As we have already described, if you stop and consider what you are doing when you compose text for an email, for example, you notice that you are imagining saying these sentences to the person to whom the email will be sent. The process of writing does not occur in an abstract inner world of ideas but is a process of formulating speech/writing acts within the imagined context of the person to whom the message is to be sent.

Thus, we are not simply a body and brain that acts alone in a void, but rather brain-body agents that interact with many sorts of specific contexts. Even in the moments when we are contemplative and thinking without seeming to be anywhere doing anything particular, our thinking is constituted by imagined actions and experiences embedded in the sorts of situations that we have experienced at some prior time or can imagine in the future. It is not possible for us to think about ourselves extracted from the particular contexts of our unique personal history, or what future situations that history allows us to imagine.

THE EMBODIED AND EMBEDDED SELF

If the soul/mind is embodied, so also is what we imagine to be our "self." Embodied and situated cognition suggests that our idea of our self is built on the actions of our body in the world—the physical world and the social world. It involves records and schemas of our history of being an actor within the different contexts in which we have been embedded. "I" am this body that has this particular history of being an active agent in these contexts and with this particular imagination for the possibilities for my future action.

Within the body-soul dualism of the Cartesian understanding of human nature, my "self" is a nonmaterial reality inside of me, equivalent to or over-lapping with my inner soul and/or mind.[32] In the world of Cartesian materialism, where thinking is a computer-like process of manipulating symbols that

---

[32]The list of terms here depends on the particular philosophical understanding. Our view is that these are all different ways of talking about the many capacities and properties of a highly complex, but undivided, human being.

are abstract representations of the world, the "self" is a data set that is abstracted into a semantic category that is labeled "me." In the world of embodied cognition, thinking and knowing occur through simulations based on memories of situations in which one has acted. Thus, to know myself is to know what I have done in the past and what these actions felt like and what impact they made on the physical or social world in which I was embedded. To know myself is also to know (simulate) what I can imagine myself doing in the future, and what impact I might have in various imagined situations. To know myself is to know a knower that knows itself (and others) by simulations of remembered bodily interactions. It is in this light that theologian Phil Hefner and his colleagues refer to a person as a "bodyself."[33]

This leads to an important additional point—the agent that we each come to know as "me" acts somewhat differently within the different contexts in which we are embedded. We are detectably different persons in context X and in context Y because the actions that constitute us are situated—they are done with respect to the particular demands of the specific situation. Our selves are specific to different contexts. Imagine yourself at a professional sporting event. The context evokes particular feelings (e.g., warm feelings toward your team and disparaging feelings toward your opponent), thoughts, and behaviors (e.g., shouting, jumping up and down, eating and drinking, high-fiving) that are specifically appropriate to that context. There is a sense of body-self that is evoked by the sporting event. Now imagine yourself in a church service. This context will evoke entirely different feelings, thoughts, and behaviors. If your sense of self was not contextually situated you could be seriously embarrassed when you shouted your feelings about the sermon or high-fived other parishioners! Embodied cognition suggests that these changes in you are not the outcome of your abstract conscious thinking about the type of behavior that is allowed in each situation but are the embodied consequences of the situation itself (learned from past experiences). The situation selects the version of you that will emerge.

Of course, there are very significant consistencies and similarities (hopefully) in the "me" that is the agent nested in the various contexts, but a self

---

[33]Philip Hefner, Ann Milliken Pederson, and Susan Barreto, *Our Bodies Are Selves* (Eugene, OR: Cascade Books, 2015).

cannot be extracted (or abstracted) from its embeddedness in contexts. In some sense, then, "self" is not something we *have* or *are* but is something that is *evoked* via our memories of what we did, or tend to do, in the context of the situations of our lives. We don't have a self as much as we "selve." And because of our ever-changing embeddedness in various situations, different sorts of selves (self-experiences) can be evoked in different contexts.

Central to the embeddedness that evokes different self-experiences is interpersonal relationships. The most important contexts in which human persons are situated are interpersonal and social. Our sense of personhood is largely constituted by the impact of our interactions with others. Therefore, what we know of our selves is known through our history of interactions with, and feedback from, other persons. As the Russian psychologist Lev Vygotsky put it, "It is through others that we become ourselves."[34]

Philosopher Charles Taylor proposes the idea that humans are fundamentally dialogic selves—persons set within a "web of interlocution."[35] The idea of dialogue and interlocution for Taylor is meant to encompass a broad range of human interactions, including (but also extending beyond) language-based conversations. Without taking into consideration the other with whom we are in dialogic relationship, it is hard to conceive of what it is to be a self. Thus, our existence as selves is fundamentally relational—that is, dialogic. Personhood is inherently relational. A self is a body whose actions are embedded in, and contextualized by, a community. We cannot imagine our selves outside of, or beyond, or abstracted from, our place in relational human networks.[36]

EMOTIONS AND INNER EXPERIENCES

A critical part of what makes it seem that we are a private soul, mind, or self hidden within our body is our experience of affective states and emotions. When we are afraid, sad, depressed, happy, or joyful, we experience these bodily emotions as events within us, and as uniquely our own in that they happen within our particular mind and body. Although others may seem to

---

[34]Lev S. Vygotsky, *The Genesis of Higher Mental Functions*, vol. 4 of *The History of the Development of Higher Mental Functions*, ed. Robert W. Rieber (New York: Plennum, 1987), 97-120.
[35]Charles Taylor, *Sources of the Self: The Making of Modern Identity* (Cambridge, MA: Harvard University Press, 1989).
[36]The reader can imagine how this relates to the issues of poverty, racism, exposure to violence.

be the cause of an emotion, and the emotion may be evident to others on our face or in our body posture, nevertheless we understand these as entirely our own and about us.

The model of spirituality that focuses on the quality of inner subjective experiences rests heavily on feelings—such as inner feelings of blessedness, harmony, gratitude, guilt, or abandonment. Much of what we read in the Psalms beautifully expresses such affective states and experiences. These experiences are valid and important. However, there are critical questions to consider about affective states, such as whether they are disembodied states, and whether they are most accurately understood as entirely our own, and whether they are indices of our individual spiritual status or well-being.

A closer look at emotions suggests that they are not entirely about us or completely inward events. In their essence, emotions are not private, person-only events but are means of *inter*personal coordination. Emotions allow us to signal to others our behavioral dispositions and to read the dispositions of others.[37] In this sense, philosopher Paul Dumouchel describes emotions as *interdividual* rather than individual.[38] That is, our emotions always involve more than one person. Thus, emotions are a communication medium with respect to our intentions; and the bodily expressions of the emotions of the other provide important information about their intentions toward us or the present situation. Thus, an important contribution to the coordination of ongoing interpersonal relationships occurs through the medium of bodily emotions. Emotional communication and attunement between people are mediated bodily by posture, facial expression, vocal tone, and even the diameter of the pupil of a person's eyes.

Emotions are also complexly modulated states of our body that prepare us for actions (such as fight or flight). Because they are bodily processes, our experiences of our own emotions, as well as our detection of the emotions of others, are in most cases quite subtle and below the level of our awareness. We are only consciously aware of our more salient emotional states that occur

---

[37]This view of emotion is expressed well in Paul Dumouchel, "Emotions and Mimesis" in *Mimesis and Science: Empirical Research on Imitation and the Mimetic Theory of Culture and Religion*, ed. Scott R. Garrels (East Lansing, MI: Michigan State University Press, 2011), 75-86.

[38]Dumouchel, "Emotions and Mimesis," 79.

when there is some discontinuity in the flux of interpersonal coordination and attunement. Thus, it is also true that emotions are not on-and-off experiences but are continuous bodily states of resonance or discord with our physical or social environment.

Imagine two individuals approaching each other to engage in conversation. Each is involved in an immediate read of the other person: facial expression, body posture, rate of walking, direction of gaze, etc. From this information each knows something about the intentions of the other with respect to the interaction. If, as the individuals approach, one person is calm and the other is distressed about something, they each detect these emotions in the other and implicitly adjust themselves based on the perceived state/intentions of the other. This is a rapid, unconscious, and reciprocal process. Because of the tendency of individuals to imitate each other's behaviors, there is also a strong tendency for emotional contagion. One person's emotions and behavior begin to affect the other, such that eventually both become more emotionally synchronous, experiencing the same emotion.[39]

Because emotions are means of attunement with others, at times we can experience emotional contagion across entire groups. Inter-individual emotional adjustments can get spread across a larger interactive network of persons such that all begin to experience the same emotion as each attunes to the dominant emotion of the group. This can, of course, be dangerous (as in mob behavior) but can also be uplifting (as in the experience of singing together) or exciting (as we might experience at a basketball game).

If emotions are bodily states of interdividual attunement, and are an important source of our experience of having an inward self, what is the nature of affective experiences when we are alone and not in the company of other individuals—for example, experiences associated with seemingly private devotional practices? We have described elsewhere, and will redescribe as we progress in this book, the nature of thought as constituted by running embodied simulations of past life experiences, as well as simulations of potential future actions and interactions. Much of thought is constituted by simulations of speaking—to ourselves, to particular others, or to God. These simulated

---

[39]Emotional contagion and its relationship to mirror neurons is discussed by Christian Keysers, *The Empathic Brain*, 92, 94.

actions and interactions include emotional attunements with imagined others, the consequences of which communicate to our consciousness (if we choose to pay attention to them) through our bodily responses linked to the ongoing simulation. Thus, internal feelings (affective states) associated with religious devotional times are not disembodied (evidence of an inner spirit or soul), nor are they entirely individual; rather, they are the embodied feelings attached to the *interdividual* simulations that comprise our thoughts and prayers. What they signal to us is the bodily affective tone of the content of our current action-simulations that constitute our prayers.

MINDS BEYOND BODIES

IN CHAPTER THREE, WE REVIEWED arguments for the view that persons and their minds are embodied. We proposed a view of persons as highly complex (hypercomplex) physical organisms with genuine capacities for rationality and relationality. We also dealt with the embodied *content* of mental processes—that is, the idea that we think via simulations of bodily interactions with the world. We considered the idea that persons are always situated in some context with which they are interacting. Minding cannot be abstracted from interacting. Our particular focus was how our bodies are deeply implicated in our thinking and emotions and sense of self. We also considered how much our bodies are the basis of our internal feelings and our capacity to appreciate the feelings of others. Finally, we described how emotions (feelings of the current status of our bodies) are deeply social—interdividual, not individual.

The concept of an embodied and situated person, as we have described it, might suggest that persons are discreet physical bodies who are affected by, but not a part of, the surrounding extrapersonal physical and relational situations and contexts. Thus, persons are bounded by the skin, even though significantly impacted by the outside influences of the contexts within which they are situated. It would follow, then, that mind is a property of the entire body but not more than the body.

But this does not appear to be the entire story. There is speculation within philosophy of mind that a person, as a locus of mental processing and as an agent in the world, may not be entirely encompassed within the skin. The theory of extended cognition suggests that what qualifies as "mind" may involve (at different times and in dynamically changing ways) interactive coupling with things outside the body (tools such as cellphones) and/or with other people. That is, our minds at any particular moment can extend beyond our physiological boundaries. These temporary outside-the-skin soft couplings allow external things or persons to become real and integral parts of the immediate processes of thinking or problem solving, such as to be a genuine part of the currently operating mind, enhancing our human capacities.[1]

Philosophers Andy Clark and David Chalmers express the critical aspects of instances of this sort of extension of mind as follows:

> The central feature of these cases is that the human organism is linked with an external entity in a two-way interaction, creating a *coupled system* that can be seen as a cognitive system in its own right. All the components in such a system play an active causal role, and together they govern behavior in the same sort of way that cognition usually does. Remove the external component and the system's behavioral competence will drop, just as it would if we remove part of its brain.[2]

Clark argues in his book *Natural Born Cyborgs* that this process of becoming cognitively coupled with an external device or person is natural and ubiquitous for humankind. Clark argues that such incorporation of external devices into our mental processing systems is relatively unique to humans and an important contributor to our remarkably powerful cognitive capacities.[3] As Edwin Hutchins argues, "local functional systems composed of a person in interaction with a tool have cognitive properties that are radically different from the cognitive properties of the person alone."[4] In this light he argues that "to ascribe to individual minds in isolation the properties of systems . . . is a serious but frequently committed error."[5]

Because this idea of an extended mind is central to the thesis of this book, the next two chapters will describe the concepts surrounding extended

---

[1] Andy Clark, *Supersizing the Mind: Embodiment, Action, and Cognitive Extension* (Oxford, UK: Oxford University Press, 2011). Marshall McLuhan, in his book *Understanding Media: The Extension of Man* (Cambridge, MA: MIT Press, 1994), makes a case for the role of media in extending human life which is somewhat similar to Clark's argument. However, McLuhan is primarily focused on the role of media on society as a whole and has no concept of extension in the form of the coupling of external artifacts (like media) into the cognitive systems of individuals.

[2] Andy Clark and David Chalmers, "The Extended Mind," 1998, *Analysis 58*, no. 1: 7-19.

[3] Andy Clark, *Natural Born Cyborgs: Minds, Technologies, and the Future of Human Intelligence* (Oxford, UK: Oxford University Press, 2003).

[4] Edwin Hutchins, *Cognition in the Wild* (Cambridge, MA: MIT Press, 1995), xvi.

[5] Hutchins, *Cognition in the Wild*, 173.

cognition in hopes that these ideas will become a well-understood framework that we can carry forward into discussions of the relevance of extended cognition to our understanding of Christian life and the nature of the church. This chapter will outline the basic concepts of extended cognition with a focus on how the engagement of extrabody *tools and artifacts* enhances our mental capacities. In the chapter that follows we will concentrate on the extension of mind into *interpersonal interactions*, where reciprocal engagement with other persons constitutes an extended mind.

OTTO'S NOTEBOOK

We begin our exploration of the theory of extended cognition with an illustration. There is a simple hypothetical example of the extension of mind that is often used in discussions of the theory of extended cognition that was put into play by Clark and Chalmers.[6] In this illustration, we encounter Otto, an older gentleman whose memory is failing significantly due to Alzheimer's disease. To compensate for his failing biological memory, Otto uses a notebook to write down things he needs to remember—addresses and directions, shopping lists, appointments, jobs around the house, people's names, etc.—and uses this to enhance his significantly weakened memory. Inga is another person in Clark and Chalmers' scenario who does not have Alzheimer's disease and thus does not (in most cases) need a notebook to enhance her memory. So, when needing to walk to the market, for example, Otto consults his notebook for directions, whereas Inga "consults" her brain systems, specifically her hippocampus and cerebral cortex, which are the structures that are progressively degenerating in Otto. Her memory of the directions to the market is not something that Inga is always conscious of, but she "knows" how to find it when she needs it. Otto also knows how to find the directions, but, in this case, the source of the memory is external to his body.

It is argued by Clark and Chalmers that Otto's notebook (a tool outside the biological boundaries of his body) operates as a part of his cognitive system in such a way that its contributions to his memory cannot be logically and functionally distinguished from Inga's entirely brain-based memory

---

[6]Clark and Chalmers, "The Extended Mind."

system. What is more, (Otto credits items in the notebook as real records of things remembered in the same way that he credited in the past (before his Alzheimer's disease) things emerging from his brain-based memory systems,) and in the same way that Inga credits as real memories that which emerges from her brain systems. Otto's weak memory has been *extended* by *incorporating* something outside of his body into his currently operating cognitive system. For Otto, the mental system at work includes the notebook, at least during those moments in which he consults it for needed information.

Of course, at times Inga, like all of us, needs to enhance her memory of more complicated or less remembered information via notes written down in the past. Imagine she needs to walk across town to the library. The route is not easy to remember, and she has walked that way only one time in the past. Inga may need to consult the notes she wrote down when she called the library for directions the first time she set out to walk there (or she might consult walking directions on her smartphone). In these cases (notes from the past or a smartphone), Inga's normally operating biological memory needs to be enhanced by momentary cognitive coupling with an artifact (notebook or cellphone) in the outside-her-body space.

What is it about Otto's notebook (and other outside-the-skin-bag artifacts) that makes it a genuine part of his memory systems? Clark and Chalmers suggest the following:

> First, the notebook is a constant in Otto's life. . . . Second, the information in the notebook is directly available without difficulty. Third, upon retrieving information in the notebook he automatically endorses it. Fourth, the information in the notebook has been consciously endorsed at some point in the past, and indeed is there as a consequence of this endorsement.[7]

Generally, these are the same information system qualities that characterize biological memory—like Inga's. In addition, these aspects of Otto's relationship to his notebook suggest the automatic and habitual nature of this cognitive extension of his memory.

Thus, the theory of extended cognition focuses our attention on the fact that we human beings have the capacity to incorporate into our mental systems

---

[7] Clark and Chalmers, "The Extended Mind."

useful aspects of the environment that enhance our capacity to think and to solve problems. With this in mind, the theory makes the bold claim that while incorporated into the immediate problem-solving process, external tools (like Otto's notebook) become a legitimate part of mind—however momentarily.

MOMENTS OF SOFT ASSEMBLY AND THE EXTENDED MIND

It is not the fact that all aspects of the environment at hand at any moment are included in our current mental processes. Rather, at any particular moment, and depending on the problem to be solved, different aspects of the physical or social environment may become momentarily enmeshed in the ongoing processes that we should legitimately call "mind." The cognitive system at work would involve interactive feedback loops between the brain, the body, and the external artifact in use (e.g., a notebook) such as to constitute *altogether* an extended cognitive system. Thus, activity that we would label as "intelligent" and "cognitive" does not occur exclusively in the brain or body of a person but can also include temporary interactive coupling between these biological systems and some aspect of the external world. That is, there are frequent episodes of cognitive activity where one cannot readily distinguish between the brain/body and the tools that are incorporated with respect to the boundaries of the mind that is at work. What can legitimately be called "mind" can encompass external tools and artifacts in various ways and at different times. Such temporary incorporation of external artifacts or tools has been referred to as "soft coupling" or "soft assembly" to indicate the dynamically changeable nature of the cognitive extensions involved.[8]

The soft assembly of artifacts and tools into our cognitive systems creates what Clark refers to as "hybrid cognitive circuits"—that is, problem-solving circuits that are constituted by the tight interactive coupling of body-based and tool-based processing. The cognitive process is distributed between the person and the tool. Clark writes, "[Flexible] human brains ... learn to factor the operation and information-bearing role of such external props and artifacts deep into their own problem-solving routines, creating hybrid cognitive circuits that are themselves the physical mechanisms underlying specific

---

[8]Clark, *Supersizing the Mind*, 116-22.

problem-solving performances."[9] The human brain constitutes a "leaky" cognitive system that can actively "coopt external resources such as media, objects, and other people."[10] And, as Hutchins puts it, "tools are useful precisely because the cognitive processes required to manipulate them are not the computational processes accomplished by their manipulation."[11] It is cognitively much easier to manipulate the tool (e.g., a calculator) than it is to do the process (e.g., calculation in your head).

KANNY MINDWARE

In the previous example, Otto's notebook functioned as "mindware"—an external tool that he incorporated to enhance the capacities of his mind. Another example of mindware, similar to Otto's notebook, is the use we all make of paper and pencil when doing more complicated problems in arithmetic, such as adding or multiplying numbers with multiple digits or doing long division. Without using paper and pencil or the calculator application on a smartphone, try adding 34 and 57. You can probably do that. Now try to multiply 4871 by 347 in your head. You most likely find that impossible without extending your mental process to incorporate at least paper and pencil. Obviously, such extension and coupling with something outside of ourselves allow our otherwise puny brain-and-body-based minds to be supersized.

Since we do not have sufficiently robust internal mental capacity (called "working memory") to hold the results of all the intermediary steps in our minds, and to keep them correctly spatially aligned, we extend and enhance our mental capacities by using pencil and paper to keep track of our mathematical operations. The solution to the mathematical problem is arrived at by a progression of interactions between our internal knowledge of the mathematical processes and basic numerical relationships, and what we put down on the paper as we do the work. Our internal processes are adequate for each step, but the solution to a multiple-step mathematical problem requires action-feedback loops that typically need to include notations on paper.

---

[9]Clark, *Supersizing the Mind*, 68.
[10]John Sutton, Celia B. Harris, Paul G. Keil, and Amanda J. Barnier, "The Psychology of Memory, Extended Cognition, and Socially Distributed Remembering," *Phenomenology and Cognitive Science* 9 (2010): 521, https://doi.org/10.1007/s11097-010-9182-y.
[11]Hutchins, *Cognition in the Wild*, 170.

During the time it takes to solve the problem, our mind extends by incorporating these external implements and interactions into the internal processes such that our ability to do more complex math is enhanced. Extension to include paper and pencil may not be needed by a mathematical savant, but for the majority of the population complex math problems cannot be done (or cannot be done efficiently) entirely within the brain.

Andy Clark, in his introduction to *Supersizing the Mind,* tells about a historian finding a batch of notebooks of calculations and drawings of the Nobel Laureate physicist Richard Feynman and describing these notes as "a record of Feynman's day to day work." Feynman replied that these were not a *record* of the work, they *were* the work. "You have to work on paper, and this is the paper. Okay?"[12] Feynman clearly viewed his notes and drawings as an integral part of the ongoing cognitive processes that constituted his intellectual work.

Electronic calculators and applications on our smartphones have relieved us of the necessity of doing all the intermediary steps on paper. These steps have been programmed into the application and are hidden from view. The consequence is that our cognitive processing has now been even more significantly enhanced by electronics that replace the need for paper and pencil. We now soft couple with our smartphones long enough to get the answer to our mathematical problems more quickly and efficiently. Clark reports that youth in Finland have dubbed cellphones "kanny," which means an extension of the head.[13]

Of course, this logic can be applied to the multiplicity of ways we use computers and smartphones to enhance a great many aspects of our minds. This thought prompted Clark to suggest that to have one's laptop crash is like having a mild stroke.[14] Our computers are so much a part of our mental processing that a computer crash means that a big chunk of our mindware has become dysfunctional. Like the effects of stroke, there are now extended mental processes that cannot be done at all or can only done by laborious workarounds.

---

[12] From James Gleich, *Genius: The Life and Science of Richard Feynman* (New York: Pantheon, 1992). As quoted by Clark, *Supersizing the Mind,* xxv.
[13] Clark, *Natural Born Cyborgs,* 9.
[14] Clark, *Natural Born Cyborgs,* 10.

In this light, it is interesting to consider how much of the processes of composition that occur while writing an essay using a computer is the outcome of an extended and tightly coupled feedback system that includes the keyboard and screen (or pen and paper when writing by hand). Somewhat vague ideas are translated into words in real time as we type. We don't often precompose the sentences that we type, but we compose as we go using the feedback loop formed by the words on the screen as the context and trigger for what comes next. Besides creating the concrete form of the essay, the interaction with the text (on screen or paper) extends and enhances the mental *process* of composition.

One additional example of mindware is worth noting. If you are wearing a wristwatch and someone comes up to you and asks, "Do you know the time?" you rightly answer, "Yes." You then consult your watch and tell the person who asked what you see on your watch. If you are a person who is interested in movies and a person asks you, "Do you know who won the Academy Award for Best Supporting Actor last year?" you might well answer "yes," since you know that you know this. However, it might take a moment for you to search your brain systems to access the information; "Wait, I know it, but give me a minute to remember." Is there a fundamental difference between these two scenarios other than our prejudice that "mind" must be entirely inside the head? At the point in time that one wishes to become explicitly aware of the time or the Best Supporting Actor, is there a fundamental difference in the mental processes at work between consulting one's watch and consulting one's inner memory systems other than consulting different versions of mindware? In both cases we rightly answer that we know the information because we know that the information is available "just in time" on an "as-needed" basis. *Just in time* and *as-needed* characterize our relationship to both information we carry around in our brain-based memories and the time on our watch—as well as the notes in Otto's notebook or the phone numbers in the contacts list of your cellphone. Consulting an external source like a notebook and consulting our brain systems for information are, from the logic of an *information* system, the same sort of process. Such external devices serve to extend the capacities of our minds beyond the capacities of the wetware of our brain systems functioning on their own.

TOOLING UP FOR EXTENDED ACTION

The domain of mechanical tools helps us think further about the nature of the *coupling* and *soft assembly* involved in extended cognition and how it might differ from mere use. Driving nails with a hammer does not seem to qualify as relevant to cognitive or mental functioning. However, if we keep in mind the broader sorts of tasks that driving nails might allow us to accomplish (e.g., building a house), then a hammer is as reasonable to consider as a pencil. What is important about hammering for our current purposes is that it illustrates important aspects of the soft assembly and coupling that extends the mind. For a person who seldom uses a hammer, to begin hammering is to manipulate an external, not-yet-well-incorporated object. There is very weak (if any) soft assembly of the hammer into the motor system of the brain/body. The hammer is part of the external world, and the hammering is merely use rather than robust coupling. However, with frequent use (e.g., in the hands of a carpenter) the hammer becomes soft-assembled into the body such that the motor system of the brain takes the hammer into account as if it were a part of the body. That is, as far as the brain is concerned, the hammer becomes a functional extension of the arm and hand. Research has shown that brain maps of the body can include an implement like a hammer as if it were an extended part of the hand, and the furthest extent of the body as mapped by the brain is the business end of the hammer.[15] In fact, the hammer becomes so well incorporated that it disappears from the consciousness of the carpenter—the hammer itself becomes transparent in its use. All he or she need attend to is the nail.

This scenario is at play with all sorts of expert tool use, including expert users of sports equipment (e.g., baseball bats and gloves, golf clubs, tennis rackets, etc.). This is also true of a pen or pencil in the hands of someone who knows how to write, or a bicycle engaged by someone who knows how to ride. Or consider a musical instrument being played by a virtuoso compared to a beginner.

Even more dramatic is the incorporation of a prosthetic limb into the brain's body mapping. With sufficient use, a prosthetic limb is mapped by the brain as if it were a part of the physiological body.[16] A remarkable example

---

[15]Clark, *Supersizing the Mind*, 10.
[16]Clark, *Natural Born Cyborgs*, 115-19.

of the incorporation of an artificial limb into neural systems is the robotic third arm of a performance artist named Stelarc. Stelarc devised a robotic third arm and hand that was controlled by the electrical activity generated by certain muscles in his legs and torso. After many years of performing with the third hand, he could control the third hand without needing to consciously focus on his leg and torso muscles, or even on the hand itself. The hand did what he intended intuitively and immediately, very much like his two natural hands. The presence and control of the third hand had been so well incorporated into his brain's motor control systems that it had become, when he was wearing it, an extended part of him. "The locus of voluntary control that, to all intents and purposes, is the person—Stelarc—has been expanded to include some non-biological parts and circuits."[17]

Since the 1980s there has been continued development and improvement of human-controlled robotic devices. For example, systems have been developed for manipulating hazardous materials from a safe distance that involve a person manipulating robotic hands. A human in one location has her hands inside gloves that sense her hand movements. These movements are used to control robotic arms and hands at another location. Both visual and tactile feedback are available to the human doing the controlling. What is important for us is that the person doing the controlling has the strong impression of being present in the distant location where the robotic work is being accomplished and of doing the work with her own body. This phenomenon of experience is called "telepresence" and illustrates the capacity of humans to become so tightly coupled with an external action system (in this case the distant robotic system) that the external system becomes cognitively mapped such that the work is felt by the operator as accomplished by her own body—as a direct effect of her physical self.[18]

Such expert coupling with tools and artifacts involves brain-body system reorganization and learning such that the soft-coupling network is already preprogrammed when the tool is engaged at a later time. Once the artifact (a pencil, hammer, musical instrument, or distant robotic system) is engaged, the appropriate network is ready to run. Thus, these neural programs are

---

[17]Clark, *Natural Born Cyborgs*, 115-18.
[18]Clark, *Natural Born Cyborgs*, 92.

conceived of as having "plug points" where the external tool can plug into the cognitive network, thus embodying an extended cognitive system—"plug and play."[19] The third hand of Stelarc and the robotic systems for distant handling of dangerous materials become hybrid cognitive systems programmed by experience into the brain-body systems of their expert users with plug points ready for facilitating cognitive incorporation.

The point to be considered is that, in our interactions with the world of useful artifacts, what we credit as "mind" very often should not stop at the brain or at the skin but should include the artifacts we have momentarily incorporated into our cognitive systems. Clark expresses it this way: "Human minds and bodies are essentially open to episodes of deep and transformative restructuring in which new equipment . . . can become quite literally incorporated into the thinking and acting systems that we identify as our minds and bodies."[20]

EXTENSION AS DISTINCTIVELY HUMAN

Our capacity to map and incorporate hammers, notebooks, paper and pencil, smartphones, prosthetic limbs, robotic systems, computers, and much more into hybrid cognitive circuits for problem solving and action illustrates the dynamic flexibility and plasticity of the human brain. This capacity for encompassing objects outside the skin into the cognitive system to accomplish a task at hand is thought by Clark to be a distinctive (if not unique) capacity of human beings. Clark writes, "For what is special about human brains, and what best explains the distinctive features of human intelligence, is precisely their ability to enter into deep and complex relationships with non-biological constructs, props, and aids."[21]

We have distinctly powerful intelligence not solely due to the size and complexity of our brains, but also to the openness of our cognitive systems to these sorts of soft assemblies with things and persons outside our biological selves. We do not need to store everything in our biological memories or do all mental processes in our own isolated brains; rather, we are remarkably

---

[19]Clark, *Supersizing the Mind,* 156.
[20]Clark, *Supersizing the Mind,* 31.
[21]Clark, *Natural Born Cyborgs,* 5.

adept at knowing where information can be found (rather than needing to store it in our brains) and how to manipulate external artifacts to solve problems (rather than doing all the processes internally). As Clark puts it, "It is our special character, as human beings, to be forever driven to create, co-opt, annex and exploit non-biological props and scaffolding."[22] With respect to our capacity to incorporate increasingly more complex and powerful technology into our cognitive systems, Clark considers humans to be "natural born cyborgs." Humans are so adept at the inclusion of cognitive tools that, according to Clark, "Tools-R-Us, and have always been."[23]

THINGS THAT SUPERSIZE

Much of what we have described in this chapter originates from Clark's book titled *Supersizing the Mind: Embodiment, Action, and Cognitive Extension.* It should be obvious by now that the point of the idea of "supersizing" is that cognitive power and intelligence are significantly enhanced when, given the opportunity, we temporarily incorporate tools or persons outside of our brain and body. Compared to what is possible through extension, the nonextended mind is less potent, diminished, and relatively puny. Without an address book or a contacts list on our smartphone, for example, we are not able to remember many phone numbers or email addresses.

The paradigmatic example of supersizing is the digital computer. Perhaps you have seen the movie *The Imitation Game.* It is the story of Alan Turing's invention of an electronic computer capable of determining, anew each day, the current setting of the German Enigma machine in order to decode German communications during World War II. Prior to Turing's invention of this computer, a group of smart mathematicians was in possession of an Enigma machine but could not figure out how to determine the daily settings to decode German messages. They were unsuccessfully trying to solve the problem by brainstorming, making lots of guesses, and doing masses of calculations on paper. However, they could not solve the problem. Based on logic suggested by others, Turing's brilliant mind came up with the design and structure of an electronic computing machine. Once built and working,

---

[22]Clark, *Natural Born Cyborgs*, 6.
[23]Clark, *Natural Born Cyborgs*, 7.

his computer remarkably supersized the capacities of the message-decoding group. Since this seminal event, the scenario has been repeated over and over as mathematicians, economists, meteorologists, scientists, and persons in nearly all fields of endeavor have supersized by soft assembly with a digital computer what their isolated minds could not otherwise achieve. So much of what we know would not be knowable without the supersizing capacity of this digital form of cognitive extension. The digital computer is simply the most obvious illustration of the more general property of tools—that the tools themselves are repositories of knowledge about how to accomplish a particular sort of task.

Thus, human thinking is *supersized* by the capacity to incorporate into cognitive processes various extrabody tools. "Human thought and reason emerges from a nest in which biological brains and bodies, acting in concert with non-biological props and tools, build, benefit from, and then re-build an endless succession of designer environments. In each such setting our brains and bodies couple to new tools, yielding new extended thinking systems."[24]

However, it is not only "non-biological props and tools" that supersize our intelligence. The most powerful form of soft coupling that enhances our mental capacities is our interactions with other people. It is this idea that we now take up in chapter five.

---

[24]Clark, *Natural Born Cyborgs*, 197

Chapter
5

MIND BEYOND
THE INDIVIDUAL

THE PREVIOUS CHAPTER began our consideration of the idea of an extended and consequently "supersized" mind. We considered the idea that what is appropriate to refer to as "mind" or "intelligence" or "cognition" includes, at various times and in many different ways, our interactive engagement with physical artifacts and tools that are outside of our brain and body—outside of the "skinbag."[1] At any moment, the processes of "minding" might include a notebook, paper and pencil, a smartphone, a computer, how-to instructions, a to-do list (referred to by Warren as his "shame-and-anxiety list," and by Brad as "that thing that I need an alarm to remind me to look at"), or a host of other things that momentarily extend our mental processing capacities. We also considered how flexible and plastic the brain is in its ability to soft assemble with artifacts such as tools or prostheses that extend our bodies to accomplish particular tasks. The critical element in the incorporation of an external artifact or tool into our cognitive systems is that we are reciprocally and seamlessly interacting (via action and feedback) with whatever it is that is immediately in use. However, how seamlessly a tool or artifact is incorporated is a matter of degree in that tools, for example, that are frequently and expertly used are more tightly coupled than those with which one has little experience. Tools (e.g., bats, clubs, rackets) used in sports by experts are transparent when in use in the same sense as hands and arms. Thus, cognitive extension and soft coupling are ubiquitous but graded properties.

---

[1] Andy Clark, *Supersizing the Mind: Embodiment, Action, and Cognitive Extension* (Oxford, UK: Oxford University Press, 2011), 76.

In this chapter, we will explore the idea that our minds and cognitive capacities are also extended and "supersized" by our interactions with other people. In fact, the most robust and potent forms of cognitive enhancement occur as we interact with one another. While we consider our intelligence to be *ours* as individual persons, it is, in fact, an interpersonally *shared* capacity. Our intelligence is also enhanced by other persons via the residuals left by the work of countless others that have become embedded in our language, social practices, and culture.[2]

MINDING IN MEETINGS

Extension of the mind is most potent when what is engaged outside the physical body is another person—the power of another mind. What makes social extension so powerful is that, while engaged in dialogue, we become reciprocally linked into the cognitive processes of the other person. Each becomes an extended aspect of the mind of the other, and the cognitive capacities of both are enhanced. Hutchins states that "groups must have cognitive properties that are not predictable from a knowledge of the properties of the individuals in the group."[3]

Consider a problem-solving interaction involving two persons. Both individuals become enmeshed in an ongoing reciprocal interaction such that each serves as a cognitive extension of the other. There is then no clear demarcation between the mental processes of the two persons during the dialogue. The mental processes leading to the solution cannot be located entirely within one brain/body. A temporary soft assembly has emerged between two previously independent cognitive systems. One might say that the mind at work is extended beyond either participant into the interpersonal space of their ongoing discussion. It is the ongoing looping of ideas-feedback–amended ideas traversing between these persons that constitutes the cognitive network that is finding a path to the solution. When engaged in such dialogue, it is not uncommon to be surprised to hear yourself saying what you are saying. It is clear to you that you would never have thought of this prior to the context of the current ongoing conversation. Your thinking has been supersized in the cognitive network of the conversation.

---

[2]Clark and Chalmers as found in appendix in Clark, *Supersizing the Mind,* 231.
[3]Edwin Hutchins, *Cognition in the Wild* (Cambridge, MA: MIT Press, 1995), xiii.

To the degree that two individuals have formed a soft-assembled shared cognitive network (a genuine interactive dialogue), it is not possible to consider the cognitive system at work to be trapped within the two separate and isolate brains. It is more reasonable to consider the emergence of a single cognitive system constituted by the interactive coupling of the cognitive processes occurring within each of the participants. The dialogue, if genuinely engaged as a reciprocal interaction, constitutes a mutually extended mind. It is not reasonable to attribute to one or the other participant any solutions or ideas that emerge from the conversation.

The late Christian neuroscientist and information systems engineer Donald MacKay discussed, in his book *Behind the Eye,* the nature of interpersonal dialogue from the point of view of information systems.[4] For MacKay, dialogue represents a closed feedback loop of information processing between the participants. As in our description of embodied cognition in chapter three, MacKay understands perception and knowledge to be constituted by action readiness—what MacKay calls a person's "conditional readiness to reckon" with the world at hand. Dialogue then involves an ongoing feedback loop of informational interactions in which the action readiness of each participant is reciprocally and synchronously impacted. Thus, according to MacKay, "For the purposes of causal analysis . . . the two that are reciprocally coupled in dialogue are one system."[5]

What is most intriguing is that, according to MacKay, for each participant in the dialogue there is an unmistakable subjective experience of entering into such a reciprocally coupled relationship. MacKay points out that "the closing of the loop [between two individuals] is almost palpably felt."[6] The basis of this palpable feeling is the experience of becoming for the moment one cognitive system. There is a subjectively detectable change when the cognitive system of each person in the dialogue has extended to include the cognitive system of the other, such that the persons have become soft-assembled into a single system, with the cognitive processing benefits of supersized cognitive capacity.

---

[4]Donald M. MacKay, *Behind the Eye* (Cambridge, MA: Basil Blackwell, 1991), 144-50. This book is based on MacKay's Gifford Lectures at the University of Glasgow in 1986.
[5]MacKay, *Behind the Eye,* 149.
[6] MacKay, *Behind the Eye,* 149.

Expressed more technically, modern theories of living systems of all kinds (including human social systems) describe the possibility of a system reorganization that results in a shift from *component-dominant* to *interaction-dominant* systems.[7] In component-dominant systems, the overall ongoing processes and outcomes are dominated (and explainable) by the behavior of the various individual parts (or persons in the context of our discussion) operating individually. However, in interaction-dominant systems, the outcome becomes dominated by the processes that emerge from the *interaction* of the parts, not the parts themselves—that is, the parts have organized themselves into one system. For example, analysis of the game activity of a soccer team of six-year-olds would clearly reveal a component-dominant team in that, by and large, each child is running around independently kicking the ball toward their goal. However, a soccer team of sixteen-year-olds who have been playing together for a while would be an interaction-dominant system since each player has a role within the scheme of the team, and the team reacts as a whole. As soon as the game ends, the self-organization dissolves back into component-driven activity. Self-organization of two or more people into an interaction-dominant system is what would be referred to as interpersonal soft assembly or soft coupling.

Every week both of us gather with our respective graduate students for a lab meeting. Often the agenda involves solving a research-related problem. For example, in Warren's lab the problem might involve how to test a hypothesis about the diminished capacities of persons with a particular brain disorder. When a solution is discovered, it is hard in retrospect to attribute the solution to a single person. The idea emerged from the interactivity of the entire group. Even if one person seemed to come up with the critical insight, they only did so with the benefit of the interactive context and scaffolding of the shared thought processes. The mind that was operative during the problem solving and brainstorming was a temporary soft assembly of the reciprocally extended cognitive systems of all the participants. Of course, not every student sitting around the table at a lab meeting may be extended into the cognitive network that is operative at any particular moment. Often one

---

[7]Guy C. Van Order, John G. Holden, and Michael T. Turvey, "Self-Organization of Cognitive Performance," *Journal of Experimental Psychology* 132 (2003): 331-50.

or two are merely passive observers and not, at the moment, engaged in the cognitive task at hand. And, when the group moves on to the next issue, a new network emerges, often including a different assembly of persons.

Another example of supersizing through social extension comes from the world of science. As science progresses it is increasingly true that the cutting-edge scientific problems defy the capacities of not only a single scientist but also the capacities of any single field of science. Many advancements and breakthroughs come from multidisciplinary teams who are able to supersize their capacity for solving scientific problems through collaboration and inter-activity. For example, huge advances have been made, and are still being made, in the domain of neuroimaging—the capacity to image the structure and function of the brain of a living person in a noninvasive manner. These advances are being made by multidisciplinary interactions involving mathematicians, physicists, engineers, neurophysiologists, and neurologists, among others. Sometimes these interactions involve face-to-face meetings or conversations, at other times sequences of emails. Sometimes the collaboration is virtual, involving cognitive seeds laid down in the scientific papers or books written by other investigators who are thus only virtually present. Whatever the means of interaction and collaboration, the cognitive process leading to the solution cannot be considered to have occurred within the brain/body of a single person; rather, it emerged from direct or virtual interactions with the minds of others. It is almost never true that our thinking is solely our own and unlinked to the work of others who may or may not be present. Instead, our thinking is a matter of collaboration and incorporation. However, whether this is seamless, fluid, and effective has to do with time and intensity of inter-active feedback.

INTERPERSONAL SUPERSIZING OF MEMORY

A group of old college girlfriends gather at a restaurant after many years of being out of contact with one another. After a round of updating on the personal status of each individual, the conversation transitions to memories of college life. Stories are told that are constituted by different persons contributing different bits out of their own memories. In the end, memories of events emerge that were not, in their entirety, the possession of anyone at the table prior to the discussion. Memory was supersized (and perhaps partially con-fabulated!) by the interactive process of group recall. The interactive process of the group has served to cue memories in each other's minds and has sig-nificantly augmented the totality of what could be remembered. This process is sometimes called "autobiographical contagion"[8] to signal the very active and dynamic process of collaborative memory.

This sort of enhancement of memory through social interactions has been systematically studied in psychological research. The phenomenon is also referred to as "collaborative memory."[9] The typical experiment involves presenting persons with a series of words on a computer and asking them to try to remember them. Then the study compares the average recall of indi-viduals responding alone with the amount recalled in a collaborative process of group recall. Generally, a greater percentage of accurate recall is achieved by the collaborative process than can be achieved by individuals working independently. The cross-cueing of memories by the collaborative group amounts to reciprocal cognitive extension into the memories of others that, in many cases, significantly enhances what can be remembered. (However, collaborative memory can, in some cases, be less accurate if the reciprocal memory system overrides a more accurate memory of one of the individuals.)

The concept of social extension also implies that memory can be out-sourced to others as an efficient way to have certain things taken care of outside of one's own head, but with the memories still available on an as-needed basis. For example, a professional executive assistant might be relied on to have certain information readily available (in brain-based or external forms of memory) that exceeds the capacity of the supervisor to remember, such as names of critical business contacts, vendors, details of past interactions, etc. Memory of this important information has been offloaded by the supervisor into the domain of the assistant (as well as institutional records).

---

[8]Elizabeth A. Kensinger, Hae-Yoon Choi, Brendan D. Murray, and Suparna Rajaram, "How Social Interactions Affect Emo-tional Memory Accuracy: Evidence from Collaborative Retrieval and Social Contagion Paradigms," *Memory & Cognition* 44, no. 5 (2016): 706-16, https://doi.org/10.3758/s13421-016-0597-8.
[9]Suparna Rajaram and Luciane P. Pereira-Pasarin, "Collaborative Memory: Cognitive Research and Theory," *Perspectives on Psychological Science* 5, no. 6 (2010): 649-63, https://doi.org/10.1177/1745691610388763.

EXTENDED MINDS WITHIN FAMILIES

Some forms of interpersonal extension are deeper, more habitual, and more implicit. Consider the frequently soft-assembled cognitive entity that is a married couple. Often each spouse in a couple that has been married for a long time has come to have the other deeply included and mapped into the cognitive system which embodies their personhood such that various forms of the soft assembly of their interactive cognitive processing have become habitual and unconscious. In different contexts and in different ways, each is an extension and cognitive enhancement of the other. For each person, the cognitive map of themselves as an agent incorporates the other with respect to habits of extended minding. These habits of soft assembly are readily re-engaged in their daily interactions, sometimes becoming virtual as one imagines the likely responses of the other to a particular situation.

One example of sharing cognitive load that is typical of many married couples is remembering important past or future events. Sometimes the extension of memory served by one person for the other is rather explicit. It is not unusual for one to rely on the other for specific domains of memory—as in, "My wife remembers all the family birthdays." When this man needs to remember a family birthday he consults his wife—a scenario very much like Otto's notebook. In the case of older couples where one is suffering from cognitive impairment (like Otto), the other can provide a form of cognitive reserve for their impaired spouse in the form of an extrabody extended memory resource. However, in most domains of life the spouses are not consciously aware of their cognitive reliance on the other with respect to the ways they cope with the many exigencies of life, including important memories.

Entire families (nuclear, blended, extended, etc.) also serve as dynamically fluctuating sources of cognitive and social extension for the family members. This is most obvious in the case of children. Young children are particularly dependent on the enhancement of their capacities of understanding and coping via extension to other family members. This is a part of what it means to develop as a person within a family. Moments of cognitive extension through soft coupling with a family member might allow for the solution of the problem at hand, as well as occasions for learning of new information and capacities. Children also learn which are the most useful forms of soft assembly and extension for solving particular sorts of problems—that is, who can help with what issues. These experiences of family-based cognitive extension are incidences of formation, allowing the outcome of the cognitive extension to be assimilated into their skills, understandings, and worldview.

As teenagers begin to differentiate themselves from their families, they sometimes pay a price in abandoning many important opportunities for family-based cognitive and social extension. Solo functioning, as if they are now entirely cognitively independent individuals, or cognitive extensions involving similarly inexperienced peers, can lead to reduced capacities to cope with the complexities of everyday life, risky behaviors, and even jeopardy to their capacity to thrive. While most teenagers are still situated within their families, they may not be sufficiently cognitively engaged—that is, they may be unwilling to soft assemble with others in problem solving to benefit from the extended mind available in family relations.

As philosopher Alasdair MacIntyre understands it, social cognitive extension is important for establishing virtues in our children (and in ourselves) and for correcting both our intellectual and moral errors. As he writes, "But the acquisition of the necessary virtues, skills, and self-knowledge is something we in key part owe to those particular others on whom we have depended. . . . For we continue to the end of our lives to need others to sustain us in our practical reasoning." He continues, "And our intellectual errors are often, although not always, rooted in our moral errors. From both types of mistake the best protections are friendship and collegiality."[10]

LANGUAGE AS A TOOL FOR SOCIAL EXTENSION

Language enlarges and transforms mind. Most of what we can think about, and how we think, emerges from our capacity for language. Whether involving real-time interactions with others or internally simulated speech, the nature and scope of the cognitive processing involved are both enlarged and transformed by language. Most of the forms of the social extension of thought and mind involve language. Clark summarizes the importance of language as follows, "Again and again we use words to focus, clarify, transform, offload,

---

[10] Alasdair MacIntyre, *Dependent Rational Animals: Why Human Beings Need the Virtues* (Chicago: Open Court, 1999), 96.

and control our own thinking. Understood in this way, language is not simply an imperfect mirror of our intuitive knowledge. Rather, it is part and parcel of the mechanism of reason itself."[11] Part of the reason that language is so deeply implicated in social extension is that it always implies some form of immediate or virtual interpersonal interaction; even the language used in the text you are reading implies an interaction (and cognitive coupling) between you as a reader and us as authors.

Thus, the depth and richness of cognitive extensions involving other persons is built on the capacities of human beings to speak and understand language. Language is dependent for its origin and development on an interactive social environment. It is a tool of cognitive extension that is learned, maintained, and progressively enriched by social interactions. In a well-known story from developmental psychology, Genie was a child who had suffered severe social isolation by abusive parents until she was discovered at the age of thirteen.[12] Deprived of social interactions with parents or others, she failed to develop language capacity. Consequently, Genie was cognitively deficient, not because of any congenital or acquired brain damage but because of her severe limitations of language, and thus the absence of language-based cognitive enhancement.

The need for language to provide a medium for cognitive enhancements through social interactions is illustrated in the emergence of Nicaraguan Sign Language.[13] In 1980 the country of Nicaragua created their first ever vocational school for the deaf. The official curriculum at this boarding school involved lip reading and some fingerspelling of Spanish words. However, the children had a strong need to communicate with each other more efficiently and deeply in the schoolyard, so they began gesturing. After a few years the gesturing began to morph into a more standardized language-like form—an invented-on-the-fly sign language. As this language of gesture was passed on to new and younger children entering the school, it began to take on even more standardized grammatical forms. By the late 1980s this phenomenon

---

[11] Andy Clark, *Being There: Putting Brain, Body, and World Together Again* (Cambridge, MA: MIT Press, 1997), 207.
[12] Susan Curtiss, *Genie: A Psycholinguistic Study of a Modern-Day "Wild Child"* (Boston: Academic Press, 1977).
[13] Ann Senghas, Sotaro Kita, and Asli Özyürek, "Children Creating Core Properties of Language: Evidence from an Emerging Sign Language in Nicaragua," *Science* 305 (2004): 1779-82.

came to the attention of linguists, who found that this system of gestures and signs already had most of the characteristics of a formal language. Thus, the spontaneous development of a new language was driven by the needs of the children for social interaction and for the benefits of greater cognitive enhancement through the richer soft-coupling medium of language.

INTERPERSONAL MEANING MAKING

What is it about the capacity to converse with another person that created the motivation of the deaf children in the Nicaraguan school to spontaneously invent together a new sign language? What is it about having a language with which to converse that can enhance thought and mind?

Recent theories in the philosophy of language emphasize the importance of coordinated processes of language interactions in the process of meaning making.[14] These theories emphasize the idea that the description and characterization of linguistic interactions cannot be limited to the notion that each individual is attempting to communicate an idea in their own mind to the mind of the other. Rather, language interactions involve a process of interactive and coordinated meaning making for both (all) participants. The interpersonal soft coupling inherent in the dialogue is best understood as constituting a self-organizing, interactive dynamical system, from which emerges meanings that are co-constructed by the participants.

It is clear from research in psychology that persons engaged in conversation become entrained and synchronized with one another in a number of different ways: body sway, posture, speech rate, tone of voice, vocal intensity, pausing, where each participant looks, and emotional contagion.[15] Thus, participants have soft coupled such as to form a "joint action system"—that is, a dynamical interactional system that transcends the individuals.

A conversation involves joint shaping and coordination of meanings around what is being discussed (both explicitly and implicitly). Coupled with the idea that the semantics of words are embodied (i.e., rooted and held in

---

[14]Elena Cuffari, "Keep Meaning in Conversational Coordination," *Frontiers in Psychology* 5 (2014): 1397, www.frontiersin .org/articles/10.3389/fpsyg.2014.01397/full.

[15]See Keysers on mirror neurons and contagion in *The Empathic Brain: How the Discovery of Mirror Neurons Changes Our Understanding of Human Nature* (self-pub., Amazon Digital Services, 2011), Kindle, 92.

the form of memories of sensory and motor experiences), the outcome of the dynamic synergy of a conversation is forming and reforming embodied meanings within the cognitive systems of each participant.

A conversation is a shared *doing*—a cooperative and coordinated physical, practical, and social process. Established in the dialogue is a shared purpose, task, or direction. Thus, conversation has a functional teleology.[16] Even in the most casual and social conversation (at a party, for example) there are social/ relational purposes that are shared by the participants and that shape the ongoing direction of conversation. And because a conversation is constituted by shared teleology, it is inherently moral—that is, it has an impact on the future behavior and character of the participants. It shapes and reshapes meanings that influence the future behavior of each participant. In this manner, moral considerations are also enhanced (for better or worse) by extension.

COGNITIVE EXTENSION AND CULTURAL PRACTICES

Another domain of socially extended cognition exists in what has been referred to as "mental institutions."[17] In discussions of cognitive extension, "mental institutions" refers to culturally established procedures, practices, and information that provide the framework for thinking, problem solving, decision making, and action in complex domains. They provide just-in-time and ready-when-needed schemas for thought and scripts for action within a specific domain that represent the cumulative contributions of many, many individuals in the past. These social and cultural mental institutions extend cognition by establishing accepted practices and relevant information linked to specific topics and complex situations, allowing one to engage the situation at hand using pre-existing cognitive processes that are well beyond what solo cognition would allow. "Such institutions allow us to engage in cognitive activities that we are unable to do purely in the head, or even in many heads."[18]

Philosopher Shaun Gallagher describes the legal system as an example of a mental institution that socially extends cognition. The institution of legal information, procedures, practices, and precedents is the product of many

---

[16]Cuffari, "Keep Meaning in Conversational Coordination."
[17]Shaun Gallagher, "The Socially Extended Mind," *Cognitive Systems Research* 25-26 (2013): 6.
[18]Gallagher, "The Socially Extended Mind," 6.

minds and previous human interactions that together constitute a system that transcends any particular individual. To solve legal problems requires access to a system that cannot be held within the mind of a single individual. As Gallagher describes it, "If we are justified in saying that working with a notebook or a calculator is mind-extending, it seems equally right to say that working with the law, the use of the legal system in the practice of legal arguments, deliberation and judgment . . . are mind extending."[19]

Accessing the mental institution of the legal system is like following directions in assembling Ikea furniture. To solve the problem and figure out what to do next one needs the benefit of cognitive extension into the minds of those who designed the furniture, as mediated through the instructions. Medicine and the healthcare system, the many domains of science and academic disciplines, architecture, etc. are all mental institutions that provide resources for cognitive extension for persons in these fields.

Consistent with our earlier illustration of the family, Gallagher speculates that developmentally the first institution that children employ for cognitive extension is the family. As he suggests, "Basic embodied and situated processes of primary and secondary intersubjectivity pull the infant into cognitive habits that shape all further learning, and that become linguistic (and narrative) practices that are further elaborated by other social institutions encountered by the child."[20] Cognitive extension into the mental institutions of family knowledge and procedures is only one of many implicit social-cognitive systems that we rely on to sculpt and enhance our everyday behavior, thinking, and problem solving.[21]

PSYCHOTHERAPY AS SOCIAL COGNITIVE EXTENSION

The social interactions and "mental institutions" (like family) that extend cognition and form our "cognitive habits" (to use Gallagher's terminology) are not always psychologically healthy. Sometimes the cognitive habits that we assimilate are not conducive to our happiness and extend cognition in ways that do not lead to flourishing. In such cases alternative forms of social

---

[19]Gallagher, "The Socially Extended Mind," 6.
[20]Gallagher, "The Socially Extended Mind," 7.
[21]We take up the issues of mental institutions and Christian life more completely in chap. 8.

cognitive extension, such as psychotherapy, may be helpful in re-forming cognitive habits. Thus, psychotherapy (which itself is part of the larger mental institution of psychology) can be thought of as a form of social cognitive extension in which, during a therapeutic session, a client and therapist soft assemble into a reciprocally extended cognitive system focused on the psychological issues of the client. With respect to therapy and many other forms of social extension, the interaction at any time or with respect to any particular topic may not be symmetrical, with both persons in dialogue contributing to the same extent.[22] Nevertheless, the relating is reciprocally extended in that each is interactively engaged in the thinking of the other. In fact, writer and psychotherapist Lewis Aron describes the therapeutic relationship as mutual but asymmetrical.[23]

While the impact of embodiment and embodied cognition is gaining more discussion in psychotherapy circles, there has been little written about the role of cognitive extension in the therapy process. Nevertheless, therapists have written extensively about the importance of the "therapeutic relationship." The quality of the therapeutic relationship is considered one element of what are referred to as the "common factors" which predict therapeutic outcomes regardless of the mode of therapy employed. The stronger this relationship, the better the outcome.

Theories about what exactly is meant by the therapeutic relationship, and why it is so important, vary widely. Some psychotherapy approaches are based on a medical model in which the therapist serves as an expert to whom the patient or client (consumer) comes for advice. From this approach, the therapeutic relationship simply needs to create sufficient warmth and trust for the patient to follow through on any and all directives (prescriptions and homework) offered by the therapist. Nevertheless, a form of social extension occurs as the client engages the cognitive system of the therapist in a problem-solving mode.

However, contemporary therapies which focus more on personality/character change than mere symptom reduction tend to conceptualize the therapeutic relationship as a more intensely reciprocal process. Therapy is not

[22]Warren S. Brown, "Cognitive Contributions to Soul," in *Whatever Happened to the Soul: Scientific and Theological Portraits of Human Nature*, ed. Warren S. Brown, Nancey Murphy, and H. Newton Malony (Minneapolis, MN: Fortress, 1998), 99–126.
[23]Lewis Aron, *A Meeting of Minds: Mutuality in Psychoanalysis* (Hillsdale, NY: The Analytic Press, 1996).

simply the consumption of advice offered by a sage mental health professional. Therapy is a mutual and reciprocal process, albeit with a somewhat asymmetrical aspect.[24] Thus, when therapy goes well, it is dialogical in nature—that is, it is constituted by a particular kind of linguistic interaction. "The dialogical is the expression of a special kind of relationship in which our interaction embraces the wholeness of the other by imagining what is real for [the other]."[25] For true dialogue and subsequent healing to occur, these theorists suggest that a third reality must emerge—sometimes referred to as "the between."[26] In agreement with contemporary work in infant observational research and attachment theory, this approach sees humans as emerging into full personhood only in and through relationships with other human beings. Thus, therapy becomes a unique kind of meeting between persons that creates the opportunity for change and transformation to occur.

This unique "between" has also been described by contemporary thinkers as a "meeting of the minds,"[27] "the Third,"[28] and "intersubjectivity."[29] Although these writers would emphasize different aspects and qualities of the dialogical moment, what seems to be the common thread is that something unique is created when the subjectivities of two persons interact in particular kinds of ways.

In keeping with our understanding of cognitive extension, we would not conceptualize this phenomenon as the emergence of a reified third *thing*, or even a third *mind*. Rather, we would emphasize that the intense, dynamical soft coupling of the mental processes of the therapist and client results in a supersized process that is more than the cognitive processing that could occur within the mental system of either participant alone. The dialogical process is not just a meeting of two minds, or two subjectivities interacting with one another; nor is it a completely new thing—a third mind. Rather a *new form of mind* has emerged for both therapist and client—a soft-coupled, reciprocal, and therefore supersized mind. The minds of both therapist and

---

[24] Aron, *A Meeting of Minds*.

[25] William G. Heard, *The Healing Between: A Clinical Guide to Dialogical Psychotherapy* (San Francisco: Jossey-Bass, 1993), 23.

[26] Heard, *The Healing Between*, 26.

[27] Lewis Aron, *A Meeting of Minds*.

[28] Jessica Benjamin, "Beyond Doer and Done To: An Intersubjective View of Thirdness," *The Psychoanalytic Quarterly* 73 (2004): 4-56.

[29] Donna M. Orange, George A. Atwood, and Robert D. Stolorow, *Working Intersubjectively: Contextualism in Psychoanalytic Practice* (Hillsdale, NJ: The Analytic Press, 1997).

patient are truly extended into "the between" of the dialogue, resulting in enhanced cognitive processing (both conscious and unconscious).

Of course, not all therapies or therapy moments are equally successful in engendering robust extension into a dialogically extended mind. For soft assembly and social cognitive extension to occur, the two individuals must be engaged in an interactive feedback loop that encompasses each other—a loop between two brain/bodies that are embedded in the ongoing dialogue. And while it is certainly possible to conceptualize this as happening primarily in and through language, it also involves empathic and emotional coordination between the participants,[30] where there is synchrony in the emotional qualities of the interaction. In therapy, as in all human interactions, the supersizing comes about through interactional reciprocity involving many forms: language, gesture, body language, imitation, and emotional expressions.

This view of the nature of psychotherapy has great importance because of its similarity (although with different goals) to Christian relational practices such as spiritual direction. Spiritual direction, classic discipleship, and small groups, designed to promote formation and Christian maturity, are relationally similar to psychotherapy.[31] These relationships should not be understood simply as ways to disseminate information or engender private subjective experiences. Rather, embodied and extended cognition suggests that Christian growth and maturity can only emerge based on the nature of interpersonal interactions—true inter-individual soft coupling. For supersizing of Christian life to occur there must be sufficient time and intensity in the relationships to allow many iterations of reciprocal interpersonal exchange. Development of a common understanding and interpersonal resonance that fosters Christian formation can only occur in the intensity of shared lives, allowing "the between" of the relationship to emerge. An extended and supersized mind will emerge between the two individuals that will enhance the possibility for formation, leading to a more robust, embodied, and holistic form of Christian life.

---

[30]Thomas Lewis, Fari Amini, and Richard Lannon, *A General Theory of Love* (New York: Random House, 2000).
[31]For an interesting comparison between psychotherapy and spiritual direction, see Gerald G. May, *Care of Mind, Care of Spirit: A Psychiatrist Explores Spiritual Direction* (San Francisco: HarperSanFrancisco, 1992), and Alan Jones, *Soul Making: The Desert Way of Spirituality* (San Francisco: HarperSanFrancisco, 1989).

As outlined in this chapter, the idea of social cognitive extension suggests that our personhood at any moment may include other persons. When we are relationally situated, our minds include and incorporate what emerges from our interactions with others. Incorporation of other minds constitutes supersizing of our mental life beyond our capacities as solo thinkers.

Based on what we have discussed in this chapter, we shall argue in following chapters that supersizing Christian life will necessarily include other Christians, enhancing life well beyond anything we are capable of as solo, isolated, individual Christians. Specifically, this book is about the possibilities of social cognitive extension within the church—that is, the possibilities for supersizing Christian life by interpersonal extensions into a body of believers. Important to what we develop in further chapters is the concept of plug points that allow for easy and readily accessible soft coupling, particularly as these are available within the interpersonal, conversational, and corporate life of Christians and of the church. Our thesis, to be explored in the chapters that follow, is that Christian life will be diminished and puny when lived and experienced apart from others, particularly when compared to the more potent and enhanced (supersized) life possible when we dwell within networks of social extension that constitute the body of Christ.

Section Three

THE NATURE OF THE CHURCH

IN SECTION TWO WE DESCRIBED current ideas about the extended nature of the human mind that demand a reimagining of the nature of Christian life and the role of the church. In section three we reimagine Christian life and the church by considering the implications of the extension of mind for rethinking the role of the church in enhancing this life. In chapter six (The Church and "My Spirituality") we begin with a discussion of the church. We begin with the church out of the conviction that the core of Christian life (and what is often referred to as spirituality) is not personal and private, but corporate and shared. While many people would begin with individual Christian life and then move to the church, the church is our first concern. Christian life, as we understand it, emerges out of the life of a body of believers, which in turn forms individuals as they extend into the body.

Chapter seven (The "Individual" Life of the Christian) then discusses the outcome of this corporate life in the formation of individual persons. A core question of this chapter is how much of what is taken to be an individual Christian life (including personal devotional practices) is actually a product of corporate life. In chapter eight (The Wikis of Christian Life) we take up the issue of the "mental institutions" that enhance our Christian lives. These include, among other things, the traditions and practices through which the historical life of the church has left resources for the extension of Christian life.

Chapter nine takes up some dangling issues with respect to what sort of church we have in mind in this book and how we understand the nature of transcendence in Christian experience. Finally, chapter ten ends this book with three conceptual metaphors that help to summarize, clarify, and contextualize the new paradigm in the understanding of Christian life that we have tried to advance.

Chapter 6

THE CHURCH AND "MY SPIRITUALITY"

WITH RESPECT TO THE UNDERSTANDING of the human mind, Edwin Hutchins argues that the internal and computational view of mind, predominant since the middle of the last century, turned away from both society and practice.[1] We will argue here that the predominant understanding of Christian life over the last century (at least) has similarly turned away from society (the church) and embodied practices.

Our contention in this book is that we, as individuals, are not as spiritual or as Christian as we presume ourselves to be. We give ourselves more credit (and more responsibility) than we should. For our Christian lives to be anything more than dwarfed and puny, we need to extend interactively to artifacts, people, communities, and institutions that are outside of ourselves. While there is currently much being said about the critical role of churches and communities with respect to Christian life, the concept of cognitive extension that we are highlighting provides rationale for *why* Christian community is important and language for describing what is happening (or should be happening) within Christian communities.

In this chapter, we focus on the church congregation at the outset in order to think about how we might understand Christian life differently when viewed from the perspective of church as a dense network of interactive extension. As discussed in chapter two, it is typical to think about spirituality, *first* and foremost, as an individual attribute of persons, and *then* consider the

---

[1] Edwin Hutchins, *Cognition in the Wild* (Cambridge, MA: MIT Press, 1995), xii.

church or community as a secondary and contributing factor. However, we start with the church rather than the formation of individuals out of the conviction that Christian life flows primarily from the church to persons.

WHY CHURCH?

There is a great deal of diversity, uncertainty, and misunderstanding about why the church is important, its fundamental nature, and what it should be about. What is the reason for, and benefit of, the worship, practices, and life together of a congregation? And even if we agree that church is primary and central to the formation of believers, what does that actually mean and look like from the perspective of cognitive extension?

In recent years a number of writers have expressed concern about the current predominant understanding of the role of the church in Christian life. Jonathan Wilson provocatively suggests that while millions of people gather weekly for church, these parishioners don't have "a clear sense of what it is that we are to do *as the church* or why we do those things *as the church*." He argues that the church exists "to bear witness to the good news of Jesus Christ," and the church is "constituted as God's people by its practices."[2] Wilson doesn't think that the good news of Jesus is best captured in a set of propositional beliefs, ideas, or theological tenets but is rather the witness of God's grace in human lives. It is faithful practice in the church and in the lives of believers that bears this out. He suggests we must understand *the church as practice*.

Wilson argues that because church is practice, perhaps we can speak of *church* as a verb. "Did we church today?" "Are we churching together?" Wilson anchors his understanding of the church as practice in the work of philosopher Alasdair MacIntyre. MacIntyre's argument can be summarized in his belief that culture has primarily given up its convictions about a *telos*— that is, the good life that is the endpoint or goal for which human life was created. Wilson worries about this for the church as well. While the *good* is particular to a given group at a given time, it is the group's *practices* that shape and form the participants toward the shared *telos*—the purpose, the good, for which they exist. Using MacIntyre, Wilson argues that practices embody the

---

[2] Jonathan R. Wilson, *Why Church Matters: Worship, Ministry, and Mission in Practice* (Grand Rapids: Brazos Press, 2007), 9-10, emphasis in original.

concept of the good, constitute the community, orient the group to internal goods, and extend our conception of the good.[3] This means it is important *how* we church. What we practice will shape us in ways that keep our Christian life either individual and limited or extended and robust—that is, will offer the opportunity for our Christian life to be supersized.[4]

For this reason, a robust and effective church must emphasize practices involving outer, communal/social, missional, and spiritual fruit bearing. As Rodney Clapp has expressed it, "those who would follow after and become like Christ give up their physical bodies to his social, corporate body, the church."[5] The church is the people who come together to be formed in holiness through participation in its life and practices—formation in the image and likeness of Christ. God saves the church and uses that holy church to create holy people, not the other way around.

Of course, individuals play particular roles in the church, but they do so as eyes play a particular role in the human body, or as actors play particular roles in a play—not themselves the center or focus or endgame, but as bit players in service of a larger production. We will have more to say about this below when we discuss the corporate/liturgical practices of the church and the church as a cognitive niche.

LIFE TOGETHER

In our previous book we began to explore why embodied persons need the church, as well as the nature of the church as body.[6] We pointed to the nature of persons as open dynamic systems that are formed in the context of social networks like the church. Thus, spirituality and Christian life cannot be understood as private and inward but as nested within a body of believers. In addition, we considered churches to be dynamic systems themselves, formed in the context of the environments in which they are embedded, but also, and most importantly, by the narrative and teaching of Scripture.

---

[3]Wilson, *Why Church Matters*, 15-17.

[4]We will say more about the meaning and role of individual practices in the next chapter. This will answer questions about how we think about these individual practices as forms of extended cognition.

[5]Rodney Clapp, *Tortured Wonders: Christian Spirituality for People, Not Angels* (Grand Rapids: Brazos Press, 2004), 87.

[6]Warren S. Brown and Brad D. Strawn, *The Physical Nature of Christian Life: Neuroscience, Psychology, and the Church* (Cambridge, UK: Cambridge University Press, 2012), see chaps. 7 and 8.

In the broadest sense, a "church" is (or should be) constituted by a particular form of life lived together by a group of believers. There are many perspectives from which to describe this life. For example, Dietrich Bonhoeffer wrote of the characteristics and qualities of Christian community in his book *Life Together*—characteristics such as praise, prayer, Bible reading, table fellowship, and work, and qualities such as humility, help, listening, forgiveness, and forbearance.[7] Bonhoeffer focused on what are undoubtedly the most important divine aspects of Christian life together and downplayed the "psychic" (as he referred to it). By "psychic" he meant individual subjective religious experiences, as opposed to the experiences of a life lived together in community.

The idea of cognitive extension helps us understand some of the important dynamic processes at play in Christian life and some of the reasons why life together is more vital than life alone. As we saw in chapters four and five, cognitive extension is the idea that we readily become soft coupled with human artifacts (e.g., tools, notebooks, iPhones) and/or other persons (e.g., spouse, family, work group) in ways that enhance and supersize our minds. Similarly, the church can be (should be) an interactive group of individuals who regularly engage one another in networks of reciprocal extension with respect to the life of faith. *Ideally, church congregations involve individuals who are regularly soft coupled to one another in reciprocal extension within the various contexts of church life, resulting in reciprocal cognitive and spiritual enhancements that make Christian life richer, both individually and collectively.* That is, reciprocal extension results in the emergence of new ideas, thoughts, experiences, behaviors, habits, attitudes, and even beliefs that are richer and deeper than we could have mustered as isolated Christians. What we as individuals believe, understand, experience, and do about our faith can and should be enhanced by the processes of social cognitive extension made possible in the ongoing life of the church.

For example, in our previous book we told the hypothetical story of Sally and Phil.[8] Sally goes to church each Sunday with the kids but can't persuade Phil to attend. Sally argues that going to church helps her get close to God

---

[7]Dietrich Bonhoeffer, *Life Together: The Classic Exploration of Faith in Community* (New York: Harper & Row, 1954).
[8]Brown and Strawn, *The Physical Nature of Christian Life*, 105.

and grow in her faith. Phil argues that he can be close to God hiking alone in the mountains every Sunday. Because Sally has a limited understanding of what her church involvement affords her, she is only able to express a few secondary individual-focused benefits of church. Sally states that she goes to church to feel close to and learn about God—that is, to obtain personal knowledge and experience. Her husband says he can have the same experiences and knowledge of God hiking in the woods. Without a concept of the possibility (realized or not in her particular church) of becoming extended into an augmented Christian life constituted by her church, she fails in her attempt to convince her husband that participation in the life of a congregation might be of more value than private experiences involving feeling God in nature.

It is important to note that social extension seldom happens if the church is merely a "loose association of independently spiritual persons" (a descriptor applicable to many churches).[9] Deep social extension and formation will not happen when merely sitting in proximity to one another in weekly church services for one or two hours per week. We have no doubt that something will occur through such practices. However, on their own such individualized worship practices will typically amount to less robust forms of Christian formation. Congregants must be purposeful in their willingness to engage and respond to each other in order for the sort of soft coupling with others to occur that results in dynamic networks of extended Christian life. If an enhanced Christian life is to occur, what is called for is *fidelity* to the call of God within the congregational life of a church, as opposed to individual *personal piety*.

In the case of the soft coupling with tools and other artifacts that we described earlier, there is an object (e.g., a hammer) and a subject (e.g., a carpenter). Social extension is, of course, different in that it is inherently and more deeply reciprocal due to the loops of action and feedback coursing between two or more minds. Thus, the benefits of enhancement flow in both directions—or, within a group, in all directions. However, although *reciprocal*, the benefits and degree of cognitive enhancement are not necessarily always

---

[9]This description of many churches was coined by Brown and Strawn, *The Physical Nature of Christian Life*, 157.

symmetric. In some interactions, the mental processes of one individual are enhanced more than the other. For example, when a person engages his or her spouse in order to enhance their memory of a person, event, or date, the benefits are asymmetric—one person's memory is enhanced more than the other's. Within Christian networks of reciprocal engagement, we must be willing to engage in interactions that are asymmetric with respect to strengthening Christian life. Sometimes the interactive coupling is mostly for the benefit of the other (at least for now), while at other times the benefit is for you and less so for the other. Different persons, and particular individuals at different times in their lives, have different things to contribute. However, all parts of the body are essential, and as Paul teaches, "the parts of the body that people think are the weakest are the most necessary. The parts of the body that we think are less honorable are the ones we honor the most" (1 Corinthians 12:22-23 CEB).

Our discussion focuses thus far on the enhancement that comes about in individual Christian life through participation in the life of a church community. There is another aspect to this enhancement that is worth noting (and to which we will return later). That is, when working together as a group, there are properties of the group as a whole that emerge. Typically, these emergent properties are more task effective than the sum of the results of the same individuals acting independently.

We noted in our prologue, and it is important to note again, that social, reciprocal cognitive extension, even within the church, does not necessarily enhance only that which is beneficial, good, or inherently Christian. What gets supersized may be neutral, trivial, detrimental, or perhaps (regrettably in the church) un-Christian. Cognitive enhancement is a *process*, not content or a final outcome. For example, Robert Bellah and his colleagues—in their book *Habits of the Heart*—argued that much of modern American life is organized around "lifestyle enclaves."[10] No doubt the interrelationships in these social groups involve forms of cognitive extension but primarily with respect to entertainment preferences. In the church what gets supersized from extension may also be more about lifestyle preferences, or political commitments, than that which is particular and essential to Christian life.

---

[10]Robert Bellah, Richard Madsen, William M. Sullivan, Ann Swidler, and Steven M. Tipton, *Habits of the Heart: Individualism and Commitments in American Life* (New York: Harper & Row, 1985), 71.

Thus, the *what, where, how,* and *when* of the extension of life within a congregation is important to keep in mind. While, as Bolsinger notes, "It takes a church to raise a Christian,"[11] the nature of the formation a church engenders in its parishioners depends heavily on what kind of narrative exists at the core of the life of the particular church. The *what, where, how,* and *when* of Christian life is established (for better or worse) in the liturgies and practices of the church. We turn first to the liturgies and then to the wider practices of the church as these provide opportunities for extending Christian life.

EXTENSION IN LITURGIES OF WORSHIP

The primary event of the life of a congregation is, of course, worship. The shared liturgies of prayer, Scripture, singing, Eucharist, and preaching provide opportunities for extension into a corporate cognitive and spiritual space. Although the events of worship are to a greater or lesser degree prescribed in a liturgy, they can nevertheless offer opportunity for joining (coupling into) a wide network of congregational interactivity. Elements of worship actively engaged in unison by a group of people constitute extensions into something greater than the individual worshiper. People who genuinely engage in (soft couple with) corporate worship extend their minds and Christian lives outside of themselves into the interactive space of worship. Engagement in the liturgies of corporate worship also extends the individual into the "mental institutions" of the Christian faith—that is, into the accumulated expressions of the church over many centuries.

In chapter four we talked about a hammer as offering the opportunity for physical extension. However, we noted the difference between soft coupling and mere handling of a hammer. If one merely carries a hammer from here to there, no coupling or extension occurs. But if one begins to drive a nail with the hammer, the hammer soon becomes an extended part of the body, transparent in its contribution to goal-directed activity (to a greater or lesser degree depending on one's hammering expertise). Similarly, involvement in worship can constitute genuine extension and coupling when we are interactively engaged in (extended into) the events of the worship. Alternatively, if

---

[11]Tod E. Bolsinger, *It Takes a Church to Raise a Christian: How the Community of God Transforms Lives* (Grand Rapids: Brazos Press, 2004).

one attends church to merely watch and listen (or watches a televised worship service) without actually becoming interactively engaged, there is little, if any, enhancement of Christian life. Perhaps in watching and listening we can pick up an element or two that is useful for our individual life and thought—which is not useless, just relatively puny.

It would seem that the move to extend into worship (or any other object or social interaction) must involve an act of the will, even if it is an unconscious act. The mere presence of an object or social situation that affords the possibility of extension does not automatically elicit the sort of interactivity that would constitute soft coupling, cognitive extension, and enhancement. There must be a move on the part of the individual to engage the opportunity. Similarly, there must be a reciprocal move on the part of other members of the community to engage the individual. Woody Allen was off the mark in saying, "Showing up is 80 percent of life."[12] Just showing up is insufficient.

In thinking about the possibility of extension and enhancement through corporate worship, it is instructive to consider more specifically the various elements in a typical worship liturgy.

Prayer. Individual prayer is a powerful practice in which a believer may sense the presence of God, voice concerns, intercede on behalf of others, receive a word from God, and even experience transformation. (We will discuss in the next chapter the degree to which private devotional prayer is not entirely understandable as a private and individual event.) But in corporate prayer—that is, prayer with others—interactive soft coupling may occur that extends the reach and power of individual prayer. The corporate prayer becomes an occasion for extension of individual prayer into a common realm of concerns, petitions, and thanksgiving. Corporate prayers are bigger than our own individual concerns, focusing on things worthy of prayer that might not occur to us if left only to ourselves, or are prayed for in a way that extends our perspective. One of us (Brad), in his role as teaching pastor at his church, regularly leads the "corporate congregational prayer" as a part of Sunday worship. Brad purposefully prays for those suffering from physical illness (a common corporate practice) as well as those suffering from mental illness (an

---

[12]As quoted in Fred R. Shapiro, *The Yale Book of Quotations* (New Haven, CT: Yale University Press, 2006), 17.

uncommon practice). By doing so, mental illness is brought to the minds of congregants who might not normally think of it—thus extending their perspective. Equally powerful in extending prayer into the entire corporate space are times where congregants may give audible voice to prayers, greatly expanding the realm of congregational awareness and prayerful concern into which each extends.

Romans 8:26 says that, when we don't know what we ought to pray for, the Spirit intercedes for us through wordless groans. In a similar way, in corporate prayer the church prays for us when we don't know what or even how to pray. In fact, it may be that the extended and reciprocal nature of communal prayer creates the very conditions by which the Spirit intercedes on our behalf.

Particularly powerful from the point of view of cognitive extension is prayer in small groups. Here prayers are typically voiced by each member in ways that are interactive. Concerns raised in the prayers of one are revoiced by another and often reshaped by their perspective. During such soft-coupled networks of praying there is often the palpable experience of engagement with others, much like our previous description of the subjective experience of moments of engagement with others in dialogue. There is also the realization of participating in a form of prayer that is beyond the capacities of any single individual. The Spirit of God is experienced most acutely in prayer "where two or three are gathered together" (Matthew 18:20 KJV).

Corporate prayer as extension and soft coupling serves another important function. Because, as we have argued, knowledge of oneself is the outcome of being embedded within networks of other persons, it is meaningful and formative to hear others praying for and with us. Even beyond what God may or may not do via the church's prayers, there is something powerful in knowing that others are praying for me, or at the very least, are holding me in mind. Crucially important is also the simple but profound sense of care experienced when someone is aware that they have been prayed for. To privately pray for one's own healing is very different from participating in a corporate liturgy of healing by kneeling at an altar and being prayed for publicly and perhaps anointed with oil.

Another important outcome of corporate prayer is that these prayers serve as reminders to the group of personal needs, which may then lead to actions that directly encounter an expressed need. For example, prayers for a sick parishioner might lead to a food chain, hospital visits, or telephone calls. While the Holy Spirit cannot be reduced to simply human action, nevertheless the Spirit works robustly through the mediated forms of intervention via God's people. God's Spirit works in and through the interactive extension and soft coupling that constitutes the life of a church body.[13] The title of a book by Claiborne and Wilson-Hartgrove poignantly captures this social extension component of prayer: *Becoming the Answer to Our Prayers.*[14] They are referring to the fact that in a sufficiently extended and interactive congregation, the body will be activated to engage in meeting the concrete needs that have been expressed in prayer.

Here are a few other examples of how to more explicitly foster prayer as corporate and extended. First, praying out loud with other believers. In my (Brad's) home group, our voiced prayers for one another are often followed by text messages throughout the week asking how things are going or offering tangible help with respect to those prayers. Another way in which prayer can be enhanced by extension into a group is by incorporating practices often used in group spiritual direction. In a small group, each shares concerns and then prays silently, waiting and listening for a word from God on behalf of the other. Sharing of these words extends individual listening into a common, more robust space. Third, some of us remember when we used to speak of "prayer warriors." These were individuals who were known to pray often and fervently, persons with whom you could share your prayer concerns knowing that the concerns would be lifted up consistently in their prayers.

Forms of corporate prayer open up the potential for praying to be enhanced by extension into the larger body of believers. In contrast, this potential can be stifled by an individualistic view of prayer that arises from a cultural narrative that encourages privacy, rewards go-it-alone heroism in Christian life, and degrades the value of vulnerability. Corporate prayer therefore should never simply be the cursory bookends that we add to the beginning and end of our gatherings when it has so much potential for

---

[13]We will speak to the issues of God's transcendence and immanence in chap. 9.
[14]Shane Claiborne and Jonathan Wilson-Hartgrove, *Becoming the Answer to Our Prayers: Prayers for Ordinary Radicals* (Downers Grove, IL: InterVarsity Press, 2008).

enhancement of Christian life as a medium of extension into the body of believers. As noted above, the kind of extension that leads to significant and deep incorporation can only happen by spending considerable time together. A one-time prayer experience is like a weekend golfer wielding a golf club. The deeper extension of a truly embodied and embedded community that spends considerable time together in prayer is more like a professional golfer incorporating a club.

Reading Scripture. Reading Scripture in worship is similar to corporate prayer. In corporate reading, we extend our thinking into the text of the written word in a more robust way. (In chapter eight we will consider the Bible and other Christian writings as part of the "mental institutions" of Christian life.) Hearing a passage read aloud by another person is qualitatively different from reading the same passage within the inner space of our individual minds. Different readers will emphasize sentences and words differently than we would. Most importantly, in hearing Scripture read in worship we are extending ourselves into the semantic context and social space of the congregational reading. While hearing the Scripture we are aware of the context provided by the reader, and by others present in the congregation. Consequently, we engage the passage differently than we would when reading it on our own. The mere act of reading aloud together gives the text a new and often enhanced meaning. It is one thing to read alone about helping your neighbor, but quite another thing to read the same passage when sitting next to your congregational neighbor who has recently lost their job. Corporate reading also engages the church as a system, shaping the properties and characteristics of the body as a whole, both with respect to its communal life and its impact on the community. In the 1960s Marshall McLuhan was famous for the phrase "the medium is the message."[15] In the context of the corporate reading of Scripture, the medium of reading together creates a unique form of enhancement of the message in which the corporate medium becomes part of the message.

In one church we attended, the congregation was made up of wealthy, middle-income, and poor individuals. One week in a Sunday school class,

---

[15]Marshall McLuhan, *Understanding Media: The Extensions of Man* (Cambridge, MA: MIT Press, 1994).

we were reading a Scripture passage about the poor. A much deeper and more enriching message emerged as individuals in the class shared about how the passage struck them from their particular social location. The corporate medium of reading a passage about the rich and the poor and their responsibility to one another came alive in ways that would not have been possible if the room was only filled with wealthy individuals or if the reading had been done privately. What was learned in the reading was enriched by the opportunity to extend thought into the context represented by the other people in the room.

Singing. Music and song have great power to move both individuals and groups in ways that transcend intellect to more intensely include images, feelings, appreciations, and motivations. Thus, from the perspective of extended cognition, singing together offers another form of soft coupling with a congregation in practices that can enhance Christian experience and life. For singing to create genuine soft coupling into the congregational expression, individuals need to be connected to each other vocally by hearing others sing, which allows a deeper sense of interaction and reciprocity. However, singing in church can at times focus on a few leaders up front, involving powerful amplification systems that drown out our own voices and the singing of our neighbor. This form of singing often occurs with darkened lighting which may cause persons to feel isolated and alone within themselves. This form of congregational singing may leave congregants with nothing more than private, individual emotional experiences that are thin and weak with respect to enhancement of spiritual life because there is little experience of joining (soft coupling) with a congregational body of singers.

Part of the aesthetic value of music is the emotions that are evoked. However, as we argued in chapter three, emotions are not indices of the internal state of isolated individuals but are clues to the state of behavioral/ intentional relationships with our environment—most particularly to the attunement of ourselves to our social context. These contexts can be imagined or part of the immediate environment, but either way they are not to be construed as entirely a manifestation of an exclusively inner and isolated state. Of course, we attune ourselves emotionally in particular ways depending on certain aspects of the music itself (rhythm, major or minor key, lyrics, etc.), but the emotions are reflections of attunement to the social context. Thus, the possibility is offered in church singing for strong emotional attunement with others in the congregation with whom we are singing. Emotional attunement to one another in song implies a coherence of our behavioral intentions, at least for the musical moment, and becomes a medium for reinforcing a rich interactive network of extension capable of enhancing Christian life.

Some Christians report preferring dim lighting during musical worship because it makes their surroundings disappear and allows them to focus on their relationship with Christ. But is this personal relationship with Jesus best encountered as an internal, private event, or is it a relationship best understood and experienced in relationship with other Christians? Our concern is that this form of worship that takes our eyes off of the love of God (who inhabits the world outside of us) *and* love of neighbor (those immediately around us within the congregation) may degenerate into individualism and emotionalism. Jesus said that everyone will know that we are his followers by our love for one another (John 13:35), not by the nature of our private affective experiences. What is more, worshipers who feel they are experiencing the moment in some internal, private space may be missing the fact that they are deeply engaged in an act of extension. What is experienced as a "private space" comes into being, and continues to exist, as a manifestation of the worshiping life of the church.

It is not just what we do but how we do it that moves something into and out of the realm of social cognitive extension. To soft couple oneself into the interactive network involved in singing together requires being able to see and hear my neighbor sing with me—to be aware of who one is singing with. This allows the music and words to become a group expression of a network of extended persons. Think about the difference between listening to a performance in a darkened theater, or singing along with a recording of Handel's *Messiah* at home, compared to singing with a very large congregation in a Christmas *Messiah* sing-along. There is an extension of the message and feeling of the music when you are joined together with an entire audience singing along. Or think about how modern movie theaters have begun to show musicals with the words to the songs on the screen and invite moviegoers to attend in costume and sing along—for example, a *Sound of Music* sing-along.

While singing has unique powers of joining people into a body, these powers should not be overwhelmed by dominance of the production quality or volume of the music. The goal should be the participation and connectedness of the congregation, not anything about the accompaniment. Perhaps traditions that don't allow musical instruments in worship have in mind something important about the purpose of music in church. There is also unique power in music that is written specifically for a particular congregation. Sermons are written to a particular body, and music can be the same.[16] While not all congregations have musicians that can write music, most can carefully select songs that thoughtfully extend the worshiping experience in particular ways relative to the congregation's context. Some simple ways to enhance connectedness through singing are choosing songs with plural pronouns, selecting songs that have touch points with the various generations in the congregation, and considering music that resonates with the theme of the day's liturgy.

Hearing the spoken word. There are significant differences between denominational traditions in how much emphasis is placed on preaching, but in the majority of cases it is an important aspect of the worship. It is helpful to consider how cognitive extension into preaching can enhance the Christian lives of congregants. Bolsinger argues that "preaching must be understood as an act of the community."[17] The preaching moment can supersize, or not, based on how the preacher and congregants enter the moment.

For preaching to enhance the life of the congregation, the preacher must first remember that she is preaching to a gathered people and not to an aggregate of loosely associated individuals. Biblical scholars have consistently reminded us, for example, that in the Pauline epistles, where Paul is translated as "you," it most often should be read as "y'all." The consequence of an individualistic misreading ("you" singular) is to understand Paul as addressing individuals (like me) rather than congregations (like us). Preaching to a people invites the congregation to hear and understand as a body and not as individuals receiving a private message from God. Thus, congregants who genuinely enter into the preaching moment do so together as a body—a network

---

[16]We thank our colleague Kutter Callaway for this helpful thought.
[17]Bolsinger, *It Takes a Church to Raise a Christian*, 98.

of soft-coupled, and thus extended, minds—with awareness of themselves as a part of a congregational body.[18] Thus, when all goes well in preaching, God is speaking to the church and not just individuals. This means that preaching is always situated in time and place. Preaching is for a particular group at a particular time. As Bolsinger says it, "preaching is always 'local talk' about divine things."[19]

Consequently, preachers cannot be satisfied with simply providing resources for individual, private spirituality; nor is preaching about making sure that laypersons get their theological-dogma ducks in a row. A sermon must be an invitation for this people at this time to enter into particular contexts and opportunities for enlargement of spiritual life through congregational extension into the work of God's reign. We have often heard parishioners complain that many sermons leave them wondering, *So what?*—a very good question, we think, with respect to preaching that does not foster extension of Christian life outside of the individual into richer domains of love within the interconnected body and love for the world.

Narrative preaching capitalizes on the human tendency to engage in mental simulations of stories that are read or heard.[20] Such preaching is an important way to foster cognitive extension of the thoughts of listeners into the world of the story as they imaginatively simulate the events of the narrative. Such sermons will likely impact congregants more deeply than sermons that simply rely on the dissemination of propositional beliefs or sermons that focus on eliciting affective experiences. Think about the difference between a sermon consisting of five main points that can be filled out in the worship folder all beginning with the letter *p*, versus a sermon that recounts and unfolds the meaning of a biblical narrative, perhaps even using images[21] to enhance the hearer's capacity to extend themselves into the story. Chances are the later message will be more impactful.[22]

---

[18]We have previously argued that a church that has entered into a significantly interconnected life together has become a genuine body in the sense that it has become a dynamical system in *The Physical Nature of Christian Life*, 123-39.

[19]Bolsinger, *It Takes a Church to Raise a Christian*, 100.

[20]There are a number of individuals who have written about narrative preaching, but we suggest Eugene Lowry's *The Homiletic Plot: The Sermon as Narrative Art Form* (Louisville, KY: Westminster John Knox, 2001).

[21]Peter Jonker, *Preaching in Pictures: Using Images for Sermons that Connect* (Nashville: Abingdon Press, 2015).

[22]We also discussed the formative nature of narratives in *The Physical Nature of Christian Life*, 118-20.

Being sent. In most Christian worship services, there is what is commonly called the benediction. In some churches this is enacted as a kind of blessing where the congregants are assured of God's love and care and faithfulness to them as individuals during the week—until next Sunday, when they return again to receive another booster shot of private spiritual blessing. In actuality, a benediction is a sending forth of the church into God's work. It is the moment in the liturgical experience when the congregation is sent back into the world to live out the love of Christ both to those who know and those who do not know Christ. Theologian Brent Pederson puts it this way,

> So God's Spirit gathers and breathes in the church to encounter Jesus Christ.
> . . . As the church encounters Christ and offers itself with Christ in the offering
> and at the Eucharist Table, the church is renewed as the body of Christ. In this
> renewal as the body of Christ the church is sent, blown out, by and with the
> Spirit to continue the ministry of the incarnation.[23]

Thus, this moment of sending should be experienced as a commission to the entire body to participate in the work of God in the world—participation that can be supersized when congregants are regularly, and often, soft coupled into interactive networks that result in work that is beyond what is conceivable for isolated and independently acting Christians.

EXTENSION AND THE PRACTICES OF
THE CHURCH IN THE WORLD

Beyond the events of Sunday morning corporate worship are the wider worship practices of the church—that is, ways in which it engages in the practices of Christian life. Thus, the sending of the congregation at the close of corporate worship should not be viewed as the sending of individuals out into isolated (unextended) Christian living. Rather, the work of Christians in the world should be understood as corporate practices that are accomplished by the whole body and thus benefit from interactive soft coupling and extension.

---

[23]Brent Pederson, *Created to Worship: God's Invitation to Become Fully Human* (Kansas City, MO: Beacon Hill Press, 2012), 43-44.

Philosopher Alasdair MacIntyre helpfully describes the general nature of practices in his book *After Virtue*.[24] A practice for MacIntyre is the doing of something within a domain of life that requires some degree of learned ability and understanding. Thus, communities of practice involve teachers and learners, with individuals filling both roles at different times. We would cast MacIntyre's concept of a practice within our understanding of the power of the process of extension of mind and action through soft coupling. An effective community of practice will organize itself in ways that allow each participant to extend (and thus supersize) their own contribution by access to the skills and knowledge of others via a network of reciprocal, interactive soft coupling. This is obviously not a one-off kind of experience, but a process—the very word "practice" implies time and intensity of interaction.

There are at least three major ways in which the work of the church in the world can benefit when functioning as soft-coupled networks of cognitive and behavioral extension. First, much of what the church needs to do to impact the surrounding community is done most effectively as shared work. In the majority of cases, the work is better conceived, and accomplished with better quality and outcome, when done as a group.

In the late eighteenth century, theologian Friedrich Schleiermacher wrote about how it might be possible to enhance the role of the church in care for the poor.[25] He first noted that, in a civil society, those who flourish within the cultural and economic environment ought to help those who are weakened by this same environment. However, the problem, as Schleiermacher saw it, was that contemplation of one's undeserved economic privilege does not elicit feelings and motivations in most persons sufficient to fuel significant benevolent action. What is more, individual attempts at helping the poor are typically not very effective and thus do not yield strong enough rewards and satisfactions to sustain the action. By contrast, when the church acts as a body on behalf of the poor, the multiplicity of compassionate acts which can occur in a group helps the underprivileged more significantly. The effectiveness of the actions of each person is enhanced when extended by the corporate acts

---

[24]Alasdair MacIntyre, *After Virtue*, 2nd ed. (Notre Dame: University of Notre Dame Press, 1981).
[25]Friedrich Schleiermacher, quoted in Michael Welker, "We Live Deeper than We Think: The Genius of Schleiermacher's Earliest Ethics," *Theology Today* 56 (1999): 169-79.

of benevolence. What is more (and here was Schleiermacher's critical point), action within a group will strengthen the intensity of the benevolent motivations and sentiments of each individual within the group, increasing the likelihood of further action.

A second way that the work of Christians in the world benefits from extension is that, in most cases, what seems to be the accomplishments of individuals are in reality the product of an imagination regarding possibilities that has been formed by some larger body within the church. The extended perspective gained in congregational life spills over into work that looks (mistakenly) to be that of a single individual.

Thus, things can (should) emerge within congregational life that simply cannot be attributed to individual congregants. Consider an example from a congregation in Southern California regarding the process of becoming collectively interested in justice issues related to immigration and the consequent effect on individuals. At first immigration was not a topic at the top of the list of priorities for most members and not an overall congregational concern. However, interaction with undocumented individuals in the neighborhood began conversations which led to a collective reading of the Scriptures in the context of issues of justice and hospitality to strangers. Consequently, a group in the church began to be actively involved with persons in the neighborhood who had immigrated from other parts of the world. This activity included development of a program to work with these individuals with respect to their legal status. Congregational interactivity and social cognitive extension around this issue fostered sensitivity and activity in individuals in the congregation that was not as likely to have emerged in the individuals without the benefit of involvement in a body developing a particular understanding of Christian justice and hospitality. Christian thinking, feelings, and doing were enhanced (supersized) within the interactive network of reciprocal cognitive extension that is the congregation. Thus, cognitive extension teaches us one very important reason why individualism in Christian life is destined to be puny—that is, it is devoid of the possibilities of enhancement through interactions within the life of a congregation.

What is more, individual actions can be significantly surrounded and supported by congregational relationships. Within a church that we know, there is considerable concern for people in the community who are living on the edge—for example, families with children who have become homeless due to loss of work and income. Much of this sensitivity is fostered by significant engagement with the families whose children attend a nearby elementary school with children from the church. In one instance, a family with several children of their own took in a recently homeless mom and her kids. They were willing to do this because it was clear they were not doing it on their own but that the church "had their back." Eventually, this began to be a burden for the host family and the guest family needed a more permanent solution. The church stepped in, working hard to find alternative housing for the family. Clearly, what seemed possible to do for a homeless family was supersized when extended by supportive systems within the congregation.

Finally, it is the sharing of stories of such seemingly individual work back to the congregation that extends everyone's imagination beyond what each person might have thought possible in their own lives. What can be imagined is enhanced when congregants consider themselves as not acting merely as isolated individuals. Thus, an imagination about possibilities is experienced in the stories of the church and becomes the basis for actions outside the specific life and programs of the church (but where the church may serve as an important backup) and is then cycled back into the life of the congregation through stories.

GROUP COHESION AND SUPERSIZING

Group cohesion is an important variable affecting the degree of enhancement of what is accomplished in such working groups and their impact on individual Christian lives. Irvin Yalom, a well-known writer on the topic of group therapy, doesn't use the language of cognitive extension, but his understanding of group cohesion would find great resonance with notions of reciprocally interactive soft coupling of individuals within a group. Group cohesion is defined by Yalom as "the resultant of all the forces acting on all the members to remain in the group" and "the attractiveness of a group for its members."[26] The greater the cohesion in a group the more likely the group will hang together, the more the members will be attracted to one another, the

---

[26]Irvin Yalom, *The Theory and Practice of Group Psychotherapy*, 3rd ed. (New York: Basic Books, 1985), 49.

more likely they will be to defend the group and one another, the more vulnerable they will be with one another, and the more they will internalize the group (i.e., the group becomes part of each member's "inner chorus"). Group cohesion is felt as a kind of "groupness."[27]

What is most important to our discussion here is that Yalom believes that without group cohesion the therapeutic (cognition-enhancing) factors of group interactions cannot emerge. One of the critical factors that can result from cohesion is what Yalom calls "altruism." He begins defining altruism by telling the following story.

> There is an old Hasidic story of a rabbi who had a conversation with the Lord about Heaven and Hell. "I will show you Hell," said the Lord, and led the rabbi into a room in the middle of which was a very big round table. The people sitting at it were famished and desperate. In the middle of the table there was an enormous pot of stew, more than enough for everyone. The smell of the stew was delicious and made the rabbi's mouth water. The people around the table were holding spoons with very long handles. Each person found that it was just possible to reach the pot to take a spoonful of the stew, but because the handle of the spoon was longer than anyone's arm, no one could get the food into his mouth. The rabbi saw that their suffering was indeed terrible. "Now I will show you Heaven," said the Lord, and they went into another room, exactly the same as the first. There was the same big round table and the same enormous pot of stew. The people, as before, were equipped with the same long-handled spoons—but here they were well nourished and plump, laughing and talking. At first the rabbi could not understand. "It is simple, but it requires a certain skill," said the Lord. "You see, they have learned to feed each other."[28]

Yalom believes that most patients come to group therapy demoralized and believing that they have nothing to offer anyone. They are burdens to others, either having been told they are "too much" or "not enough." While at first group members look to the therapist as the paid professional to offer them something, they soon realize that others have important things to share with them. They then also begin to see that each person has something to offer

---

[27]Yalom, *The Theory and Practice of Group Psychotherapy*, 49.
[28]Yalom, *The Theory and Practice of Group Psychotherapy*, 13

others via altruistic acts. These acts may include listening, emotional validation, offering support, caring confrontation, insight, and new relational experiences. And of course, like all good therapy, the goal is that this growth, which occurs both through experiencing and engaging in altruistic acts within the group, will begin to generalize outside of therapy. Extension of the individuals outside of themselves and into the experience of group altruism and cohesion is therapeutic and, in our context, enhancing and supersizing of what little was possible for the members on their own.

CHRISTIAN LIFE AS A NICHE

Yet another way to think of Christian life in relationship to the church is to consider the church as a cognitive-behavioral niche. Current behavioral biology has concluded that organisms are not easily separated from the environmental niches they occupy. The idea is that the description of the behavior of a particular organism must include the environmental niche necessary for eliciting the organism's behavior. It is often the case that the organism has a hand in creating the niche. For example, a spider cannot be easily separated from the web that it constructs. The web is an essential part (an extension) of the spider's adaptive, intelligent behavior. Similarly, as Hutchins argues, "The environments of human thinking are not 'natural' environments. . . . Humans create their cognitive powers by creating the environments in which they exercise those powers."[29] The cognitive processes of the person cannot be separated from the environment in which the processes occur. Consider Irene who starts a new business. Progressively she carves out a niche for her work and for those she hires into the business. Eventually, we could not adequately describe Irene as a business person without including a description of the business niche she and her employees have created.

The relationship between a person and their social niche is expressed well in *systems theory* in psychology. This theory argues that persons cannot be well understood without including the system or systems that encompass the person.[30] Thus, behavior that is influenced by the complex systems (or

---

[29]Hutchins, *Cognition in the Wild*, 169.
[30]Carlfred B. Broderick, *Understanding Family Process: Basics of Family Systems Theory* (Thousand Oaks, CA: Sage Publications, 1993).

niches) that the persons exist within is considered to manifest "hybrid agency"—that is, the causes and sources of actions are attributable both to the individual and to the niche or system.[31] The most important system or niche that most people occupy is their family. The behavior of an individual (both within the family and in other contexts) is often not entirely understandable outside of reference to the person's position, situation, and history of interactions within their family system. Most persons do not (cannot) act independently of influence and constraint from their family system. Thus, the niches that humans occupy (families, jobs, networks of friends, communities, and churches) are significant factors in their thought and behavior.

Christian life can be understood as this sort of person-niche hybrid. Persons do not (cannot?) act Christianly entirely independent of influences and constraints from the systems they occupy, most particularly the church. The church, and its systems of influence and formation, is often the primary factor in a person's Christian thought and behavior, such that "person" and "church" often cannot easily be disentangled with respect to Christian life. Alternatively, a person trying to live Christianly entirely outside of a church and congregational life is in the awkward position of trying to be Christian while nested (often uncomfortably) only within secular niches. As indicated above, a very critical and formative niche for most everyone is their family of origin. In some cases, the Christian life of the family supplements and stands in for (however adequately or inadequately) the absence of the extended Christian life available within a church. Similarly, the church sometimes stands in for inadequacies in the family of origin.

Andy Clark, in his book *Supersizing the Mind*, provides a helpful illustration of a physical and social niche within human life.[32] The illustration comes from Evelyn Tribble's description of the processes of production of Shakespearean plays in the Globe Theatre in Elizabethan England.[33] The cognitive problem that Clark points out was producing numerous different plays over a short time (as many as six different plays in a week), all using the

---

[31] Andy Clark, *Being There: Putting Brain, Body, and World Together Again* (Cambridge, MA: MIT Press, 1997), 218; and Andy Clark, *Supersizing the Mind: Embodiment, Action, and Cognitive Extension* (Oxford, UK: Oxford University Press, 2011), 50-53.
[32] Clark, *Supersizing the Mind*, 63-64.
[33] Original paper by Evelyn Tribble, "Distributing Cognition in the Globe," *Shakespeare Quarterly* 56 (2005): 135-55, described in Clark, *Supersizing the Mind*, 63-64.

same cast. How did actors know what to do when and where in this play versus yesterday's play, or the one the day before that? One problem, of course, is learning all the lines. However, another problem is knowing when to do what where—knowing the structure of the action sequences in the play and how one fits in.

The solution to this problem was not in the heads of the actors but in the design of the spaces and social practices of the theater—that is, the physical and social niche that extended the cognitive capacities of the actors. A consistent physical property of these theaters was a multiplicity of doors to enter and exit the stage. Near these doors was posted a large sheet that served as staging manuscripts comprised of a sketchy outline of the play with maximal attention to characters, entrances and exits, sounds and music cues, etc. Actors were not given the full text of the play but learned their lines from a minimal need-to-know document with their speeches, entrances, and exits. Based on this and the staging manuscript posted by the stage doors, they could perform their part in the play. A specific play-relevant niche had been created to allow each actor to perform their part in the grand scheme of the play being performed that day (versus yesterday or the day before).

Staging plays in the niche that was the Globe Theatre provides an apt metaphor for the relationship between individual Christians, the body that is the church, and the kingdom of God. Individual Christians are like actors. Each person is *not* responsible for the entire play but must fill a particular role. What goes on within them (their "spirituality") is critical insofar as it prompts and motivates them to know and fulfill their role well (however large or small it may be) and to do it "as unto the Lord"—that is, with the commitment of the entire self to the role being played.

Rodney Clapp describes the difference between practices in solitude and taking part in the broader practices of the congregation in this way:

> Misled by modern spirituality, contemporary Christians sometimes assume their most important spiritual practices occur in their solitude, with private daily prayer, Bible readings, and so forth. As a high school football player, I often spent fall afternoons in the yard alone throwing the football up and catching it, passing it through a tire swing, and running to stay in shape. It was worthwhile to practice alone, but I never imagined that my solitary exercises overshadowed

or were more important than team practices, let alone actual games. I knew my individual work and play derived from a pastime that was first of all social and corporate and always knew its fullness as a social and not solitary endeavor. Christian spirituality is similar. Our individual and daily exercises are important and worthwhile, but they do not precede corporate worship. They are derived from corporate worship and circle back to find their fulfillment in corporate worship. Ultimately, if others do not pray with me, Christian faith and spirituality will become small and trivial, beaten down by a world so much bigger and more interesting than my individual obsessions and desires.[34]

The physical and social niche that existed in the physical layout of the stage and the social practices of putting on plays (including the staging manuscript) is like the church. That is, the life and practices of the church form a niche within which each finds a place and a role. Christian life lived within this niche enhances the participation of each person and allows the particular group of Christians (church) to perform in the world in a manner that can manifest the kingdom of God. This metaphor of an Elizabethan play is entirely resonant with the metaphor used in Scripture of the church as a physical body with individuals having various parts—as eyes, feet, hands, etc.—each with a particular role within the kingdom activity of the body (1 Corinthians 12).

In summary, the premise of this book is that what is true of our intelligence is also true of our Christian lives. Left entirely to ourselves and our own individual resources we are neither as intelligent nor as spiritual as we presume. Much of what we experience as *our own* Christian life cannot be attributed to ourselves alone but must be viewed as the product of an extended life that is codetermined and scaffolded by our engagement with the body of Christ. In this chapter we have particularly focused on the supersizing qualities of a life shared with other Christians through dynamically varying moments of soft coupling together in worship, prayer, singing, Scripture reading, and work. Such engagement in the life of a body of Christ serves also to enhance individual Christians' lives, the topic to which we now turn.

---

[34]Clapp, *Tortured Wonders*, 88.

THE "INDIVIDUAL" LIFE
OF THE CHRISTIAN

BY NOW WE HOPE THAT YOU have caught on that (a) we think that Christian life will remain limited (what we mean by "puny") when it is understood and lived out as individual, internal, and private; and (b) Christian life can be enhanced and enlarged by outward extensions in which our thoughts and actions become soft coupled with other Christians in a manner that allows the emergence of a life that is richer than what we experience on our own. This was why we began with a discussion of the role of the church and then discussed the Christian life of the individual.

Given the centrality of the church, how then should we understand the time-honored traditions of *individual* Christian disciplines, such as private prayer, Bible reading, contemplation, etc. In chapter two we discussed the dangers of making Christian spirituality too individualistic and internal. In chapter six we focused on the enhancement of Christian life that is experienced in congregational bodies. We attempted to provide examples of how the liturgical practices of worship and ministry can extend and supersize Christian lives. In this chapter, we revisit individual practices and the nature of Christian formation to provide a framework for better understanding of these from the vantage point of cognitive extension.

WE ARE NEVER ALONE

A core idea that runs throughout this book is that humans are relational beings. Most everything we experience from conception to death includes others to some degree. We experience, learn, think, create, and imagine as bodies who are embedded in relational networks. The truth of the matter is that we are never truly alone. Even when we are absorbed in silent thought, we are mostly engaging in imaginary relations with others from our past, present, or an anticipated future. As we reflect we might imagine that particular others are conversing with us, watching us, judging us, loving us, or encouraging us. These internal others are what psychologist Sandra Buechler has called our "internal chorus."[1] While this internal chorus may impact us for good or ill, it influences us in ways in which we are not always aware. Because human cognition is not only embodied (experienced in bodies) and embedded (always in a web of social relationships) but also enacted (thought is for action), our internal thoughts are offline mental simulations of bodily, contextualized actions—mostly simulations of imaginary interactions and conversations with others. For example, you might be sitting alone reflecting on your day. Perhaps you are reflecting on a meeting you attended earlier in the day. It doesn't take much effort to grasp that even this seemingly "private" and "internal" experience involves rehearsal of memories of what happened with others, as well as a growing imagination for what you wished you would have or could have said or done, what others did or didn't do, or what you might do differently in the future. These reflections are offline mental simulations of past or potential future interactions. In this sense, then, even in our times of internal, personal thought we are engaged in a kind of social extension.

Psychologist of mind Merlin Donald reflects on our inevitable emersion in the wide domains of our previous interpersonal and cultural experiences. He writes, "Our cultures invade us and set our agendas. Once we have internalized the symbolic conventions of a culture, we can never again be truly alone in semantic space, even if we were to withdraw to a hermitage or spend the rest of our lives in solitary confinement."[2]

As noted in chapter two, in much of twentieth- and twenty-first-century evangelical thought, Christian experience was conceptualized in overly individualistic ways. For example, evangelicalism historically has placed great emphasis on the idea of a "personal relationship with Jesus." However, given what we have described about human cognition and extension, it is inaccurate

---

[1] Sandra Buechler, *Still Practicing: The Heartaches and Joys of a Clinical Career* (New York: Routledge, 2012), 79.
[2] Merlin Donald, *A Mind So Rare: The Evolution of Human Consciousness* (New York: Norton, 2001), 298.

to describe Christian life as "personal" if what is meant by that is private and not involving others. Indeed, one may have a "personal relationship with Jesus" in the form of a vibrant relationship marked by communication, devotion, and growth, but it is never to be confused with a private relationship. "Christian," as a descriptor of a person, should always imply a relationship with Christ as manifest through and within a functioning body of Christ. In the Hebrew Scriptures, God calls a people not a person (or calls a person as representing a people). In the New Testament, everything points toward the formation of the body of Christ, the church, as the medium for the ongoing, outward-focused work of God in the world. Of course, there are stories of personal encounters between Jesus and individuals, and personal decisions are made by individuals to follow him, but these are always contextualized within interpersonal histories. Thus, we should avoid reading Scripture with overly Western, individualistic eyes.[3] Personal Christian experience and life, understood as isolated, individual, and private, is in reality difficult to conceive. Only an embodied and extended Christian life makes any real sense.

THE OUTWARDNESS OF INWARD DISCIPLINES

The perspective we are describing should not be read as arguing that believers should not engage in classic spiritual disciplines, such as those described by Richard Foster in his book *Celebration of Discipline*.[4] However, what Foster calls "inward disciplines"—such as prayer, fasting, meditating, or reading the Bible alone—can and should be understood differently. Such activities are, in fact, extended beyond our individual selves in that they draw on (and simulate) memories of actions and experiences in which we have interacted with other Christians or our congregation.

For example, fMRI studies of brain activity show that when persons hear a story, their brain activity is very similar to what it would be if they themselves were acting in the story.[5] And this is true not just for the physical action of the

---

[3]E. Randolph Richards and Brandon J. O'Brien, *Misreading Scripture with Western Eyes: Removing Cultural Blinders to Better Understand the Bible* (Downers Grove, IL: InterVarsity Press, 2012).
[4]Richard J. Foster, *Celebration of Discipline: The Path to Spiritual Growth* (San Francisco: Harper, 1988).
[5]Nicole K. Speer, Jeremy R. Reynolds, Khena M. Swallow, and Jeffery M. Zacks, "Reading Stories Activates Neural Representations of Visual and Motor Experiences," *Psychological Science* 20 (2009): 989-99, https://journals.sagepub.com /doi/10.1111/j.1467-9280.2009.02397.x.

story but also for emotions described. This is why we get scared, cry, cringe, laugh, smile, etc. when we are simply hearing and/or watching a story. Our brain is imaging (simulating from our past experiences) what we might, should, or would do or feel if we were actually there. The mental processes of our "private" devotions are similarly constituted by simulations built from past experiences of prayer or Bible reading within groups of Christians.

As we have written about elsewhere, stories shape us by creating the opportunity for imagining ourselves in different scenarios.[6] Even when we are alone reading a story, we are not truly alone, nor are we passively receiving story facts. We are interacting with the story in light of all our past physical and relational experiences (with the accompaniment of our internal chorus). Narratives become a form of cognitive extension. We understand the story by imagining what we could/would/should do, or not do, in this context. By entering into an imaged behavioral scenario depicted in the story, we are running offline mental simulations of the story events, and in so doing we can vicariously try out ways to act and react in future situations.

Now consider what we have always presumed to be the private practice of Bible reading. While reading, we cannot help but interact with our own "internal chorus" of relational experiences, providing us with forms of virtual cognitive extension. In fact, some of the spiritual practices of St. Ignatius that involve the imagination were designed to enhance the benefits of what we are calling "simulation."[7] Ignatius would ask the practitioner to deeply imagine the Bible scene being read (using all their senses) and even to imagine that they are there. While this is wonderful to do as a specific practice, what modern science suggests is that we can't help but do this (though often less consciously than Ignatius advocated). So, when a Christian practices personal Bible reading, he is never truly alone or passive, but rather becomes soft coupled into the narrative in a manner that extends his spirituality through mental simulation of the text being read, and as he has come to understand the text within the life of the church.[8]

---

[6]Warren S. Brown and Brad D. Strawn, *The Physical Nature of Christian Life: Neuroscience, Psychology, and the Church* (Cambridge, UK: Cambridge University Press, 2012), 201.

[7]Saint Ignatius, *The Spiritual Exercises of Saint Ignatius*, trans. George E. Ganss (Chicago: Loyola Press, 1992).

[8]The idea of Scripture as "understood in the life of the church" helps explain why the understanding of Scripture can become so entrenched. We can't seem to understand in any different way than how we have always understood. This is why it is so important, as we indicated in chapter six, to read in community with others who are different from ourselves.

Therefore, reading Scripture when alone engages offline action simulations based on memories of past experiences, including evoking our "internal chorus." Depending on the passage and our past experiences, the inner chorus in Bible reading may represent what we have learned about the Bible from our family, important church leaders (e.g., Sunday school teachers, pastors), other religious sources (e.g., Christian books), our denominations, and the theologies that we have picked up along the way. This helps explain how two Christians from different life experiences (including different cultures) and different theological/denominational traditions may read the same passage of Scripture very differently. What emerges as we read is a virtual soft coupling between our embodied minds and our religious communities. What we believe about faith is not a product of our isolated minds but is an extension involving a simulation of reciprocal relational feedback loops. We don't believe alone, we believe with others. Similarly, we don't read alone but read with the church (for good or bad, depending on the qualities of the particular church).

A similar argument can be made regarding a number of other devotional practices often considered personal, such as contemplative prayer, lectio divina, spiritual meditation (in its many forms), etc. As we pointed out in chapter six, even if these are practiced alone, they are never exclusively individual and private. And they are definitely not passive. Human cognition is for action, and we can't help but conduct these practices in ways in which our brains are enacting behavioral scenarios—scenarios about action. Therefore, the meanings we make from these practices are in fact embodied and socially interactive meanings.

Thus, personal devotions are always socially extended by the fact that we can't help but interact with the internal chorus of our embodied, enacted, and embedded relational history, and it is from these experiences that we derive the meanings that populate our devotional thoughts. For example, these relational meanings may be from being cared for by a loving parent (embodying a metaphor of a loving God) or from relationships in which we have been taught narratives about Christian life (e.g., Christian education). These sorts of personal meanings tend also to be extended into the particular theology and doctrine of the religious tradition within which we have been embedded—

that is, the "mental institutions" of our religious lives (which we will talk more about in chapter eight).

THE COMMUNAL NATURE OF PERSONAL DEVOTIONS

This leads us to the second important point about personal disciplines. While these disciplines have often been taught as practices to be done alone, it has been easy for them to be understood simply as things to be done for the spiritual edification of the individual practitioner. We hear Christians speak about "doing devotions" in order to grow in *their* faith or to *feel* closer to Jesus. While these are not necessarily wrong, they easily lead us into having personal devotions primarily for individualistic reasons and to judging the value of the experience with respect to the state of our own spiritual lives as measured by an inner feeling state. However, if we understand and practice personal devotions through the lens of extended cognition, we must come to recognize that devotions are a form of virtual soft coupling with the body of Christ (i.e., the church). We engage in personal disciplines not for ourselves, or to feel something spiritual (although these may be side benefits), but for the sake of the church and for the world to which it is called.

In chapter two, we critiqued the predominant modern view of Christian spirituality for the ways in which it may be read as promoting an inward, private, and individualistic form of Christian life. While it is true that writers such as Nouwen, Merton, and Willard, and organizations such as Renovaré, share some of our concerns about the need for a more embodied and lived Christian faith, it seems clear that there is an important *directional* difference. These writers seem to teach that outward change in behavior follows from inward change. If there is an inward spiritual change in a Christian—that is, change in the inward state of their "soul"—then outward change will follow as a necessary consequence. It would be easy to conclude that these practices are done primarily to change one's inner spiritual nature, and then outside change will follow suit.

In fact, there are places in the Bible where Jesus seems to teach a similar idea. For example, in Matthew 12:22-37 Jesus is talking to a group of Pharisees right after he has healed a demon-possessed man who was blind and mute. Jesus warns the Pharisees that a good tree produces good fruit, but a bad tree produces bad fruit. Jesus says that from the heart, the mouth speaks. This could be understood as support for the idea that behavior will necessarily follow from the translation of an inward subjective state into an embodied action.

Or consider another passage in which Jesus is speaking again to the Pharisees and warns them that they are focusing on the wrong things:

> Woe to you, teachers of the law and Pharisees, you hypocrites! You clean the outside of the cup and dish, but inside they are full of greed and self-indulgence. Blind Pharisee! First clean the inside of the cup and dish, and then the outside also will be clean. (Matthew 23:25-26)

A simple reading of passages like these could lead individuals toward an inward, self-focused spirituality—what Owen Thomas describes as a focus on interiority in Christian life.[9] But biblical scholarship reminds us that passages like these must be read in context. To whom is Jesus speaking? In both cases he is speaking to a group of religious leaders, the Pharisees, who have linked their religiosity to the rigid practice of the law. They have fallen into the trap of "works righteousness," and thus Jesus is calling them out of their hypocrisy. Jesus is making more of a claim about hypocrisy than he is about the direction of the determinants of religious life. Jesus is rebuking the Pharisees not because they promoted doing the law but because there was a major discrepancy between the intent of the law and the consequences of their actions. The Pharisees were hypocrites because they emphasized strict observance of the outward trappings of religiosity, while neglecting the true interpersonal meaning and intent of the law and a religious life.

However, there are passages of Scripture where Jesus seems to emphasize a godly life that is more obviously consistent with what we have been describing. One of the most striking examples is the Sermon on the Mount (Matthew 5-7). In passage after passage of this teaching, Jesus emphasizes the importance of what one *does with and toward others*, as opposed to the inner state of the person.[10] In fact, in passages where he speaks of individual

---

[9]Owen C. Thomas, *Christian Life and Practice: Anglican Essays* (Eugene, OR: Wipf & Stock, 2009).

[10]As N. T. Wright suggests in *After You Believe: Why Christian Character Matters* (New York: HarperCollins, 2010), Jesus is particularly interested in the formation of virtues.

spiritual practices such as prayer and fasting, Jesus is quick to tell his listeners that a godly life is not essentially about their private good works. In Matthew 7, when Jesus talks about only good trees being able to produce good fruit, he seems to be less concerned about "becoming a good tree" (which might be understood as a solely individual state) as he is about "bearing good fruit" (an outwardly extended practice). And finally, in Matthew 7:21-23 Jesus says that many will claim to know him, but only those who *do* the will of the Father (that is, those whose Christian life is manifest in love and care of others) will enter. These teachings seem to be about an embodied, enacted, and extended faith—both what one does in the body, and whether these personal practices extend reciprocally and relationally into the lives of others. What seems clear is that these teachings are not about an inward kind of spirituality that may lead to outward good effects but about a way of being as a whole person in the world that brings life.

In Matthew 7:21-23 there is a direct link to the end of Matthew's Gospel, when Jesus describes his return in which he will judge all persons, separating the sheep from the goats (Matthew 25:31-46). In perhaps one of the most chilling passages in all of Scripture, Jesus lays out that those who enter the kingdom of heaven will not be the ones who claim to know him in some inward, personal, or private way, but only those who embodied and enacted the will of the Father and cared for "the least of these." Christian life is not primarily constituted by inward, private spiritual thriving, or by giving intellectual assent to propositional beliefs, but is rather an embodied, enacted, and extended life.

So, while many writers, both ancient and contemporary, may commend the importance of a life that exhibits the fruits of the Spirit and caring for the least of these, there is an important directional difference with respect to how this comes about in the lives of Christians. Many contemporary Christian writers emphasize the direction of inward to outward. As we have argued above, we believe this is because of an implicit understanding of human persons where the real person resides inside (in the secret inner mind or soul) and where the body doesn't really matter except as a delivery system for the mind/soul. Alternatively, we have argued that persons are neither disembodied inner spirits, nor brain-based inner computers manipulating disembodied mental abstractions, but rather bodies that are always actively embedded within a particular situational context and whose capacities are enhanced by extension into the physical and social world outside the limits of the skin.

To reiterate, we are *not* saying that personal devotional practices are wrong or that they should be discontinued. We are arguing for a different understanding and a different emphasis. Generally, we agree with Thomas when he writes:

> Thus I am suggesting that the spirituality movement should balance its emphasis on interiority with an equal concern with the outer life of the body, the community, and history. It should harmonize its emphasis on private individual life with an equal commitment to the importance of the public life of work and politics. And it should equalize its concern for feeling with an emphasis on the life of reason and reflection. In sum, it should balance its commitment to spirituality with an equal commitment to the life of religion with its concern for tradition, communal life, and involvement with public life.[11]

Our modification or caveat to this statement by Thomas would be that the "interiority" to be "given equal concern" should be considered to point to internal simulations of external, embodied (mostly relational) action in the world. Thus, we might differentiate between a view of interiority as merely subjective, experiential, and largely emotive (which we find incoherent, and which Thomas would probably not want to endorse), versus a view of interiority as simulations and rehearsals of what has been done and potentially could be done as relational beings in God's world (with their accompanying affective qualities), the value of which is measured by their realization in Christlike actions in the world.

PERSONAL (NOT PRIVATE) CHRISTIAN PRACTICES

This idea of engaging in a personal practice as a form of inclusion of what is outside of oneself, and for the sake of something larger, may sound strange to some Christians when applied to personal devotions. However, when considered in the light of other realms of life the idea may seem less foreign.

Think of activities that persons engage in alone for the purpose of enhancing possibilities in some later, more public, context. For example, imagine

[11] Thomas, *Christian Life and Practice*, Loc 1154.

practicing a musical instrument. While you may spend hours practicing alone, you are never truly alone. You only know what to practice because you are soft coupled in your imagination with someone who has taught you. This amounts to an internal chorus consisting of the memory of your teacher, or a friend that has shown you a few things, or techniques you learned on YouTube. You are also extending mentally into the larger world of music composition—musical possibilities made available to you through the historical work of others. Think also about practicing the elements of a sport by yourself. One might shoot baskets for hours alone, or hit a baseball off a tee in the backyard, or hit a tennis ball against the garage, but all this is done because you have already been shown the basics by someone else, providing you with a memory of instructions or models to be imitated. Cognitive extension has occurred in the processes of original learning, making it possible later when alone to imaginatively and physically extend into the previous instruction. Practicing without others around is never really "alone" but in the company of mentors.

It is equally true that practice alone is not isolated and private in that it is done for the purpose of improving some sort of public activity or performance. Throwing a football around alone in the backyard may develop some of the skills you have been taught, but it only takes on real meaning when you play football with others. Even so-called "individual" sports, like golf, only make sense when you are engaging in the sport with others. Actors may practice and prepare alone, but it is for the purpose of performing with others. While our capacities can be enhanced by extension of ourselves via soft coupling with teachers and models, the enhancement of our capacities in rehearsal are for sharing the skills with others. *We engage in personal times of practice that only make sense within some social niche of performance that gives them meaning.*

Now think about this scenario in terms of the personal (but not private) disciplines of Christian life. Even when we are engaging in Christian practices alone, it is not about *us*—it is not an isolated, self-referential event, either with respect to the practice itself or its ultimate value. Rather, the personal practice is an extension into the life of the church for the sake of enhancing its engagements with God's reign in the world. We don't practice them alone primarily for our own edification, nor for their own sake. While we may find them enjoyable to do alone (even as a kid likes to throw the ball around in the backyard), their meaning is only clear when they are recognized as forms of extension from, and back into, the life of the larger congregation. And the feedback loop is closed as we are reciprocally extended into the many lives of the congregation. As Clapp suggests, personal devotions are practice for the real game yet to come.[12]

This understanding of personal Christian practices as extension from, and extending back into, the life of the church has important implications. First, personal practices are indeed practice for the real game, which is living out the implications of God's reign in community for the sake of the world. For example, we pray and read Scripture alone because the community has taught us and emphasized the importance of such practice as a means of being ready to contribute to the life of the whole body.

Second, this understanding of personal practices as extended should impact the way we approach them. We don't engage in such practices by ourselves to simply grow in our own faith or to obtain emotional experiences or feelings of spiritual well-being. Recall our description of feelings in chapter six as not private, inner experiences, but as the byproduct of interpersonal attunements. When we engage in the personal practices of faith, we do so for the sake of the community—to complete and continue the ongoing interactive work. We can only engage in a practice alone because we have already had our thinking and knowing extended by the community that has taught us these practices and their value. But, since we are nested within the life of reciprocal extension, none of this is private or just "for me." I engage in the practice of prayer so that when you can't pray, I can pray for you. I pray so that I can pray with and for the community. I practice devotional prayer so that I can pray better with you. My praise and petitions, though voiced alone, are part of the corporate prayers of the church. For example, praying a lament psalm might not be consistent with my present state, but I know that in the body there are brothers and sisters lamenting. And I practice both personal and corporate prayer for the sake of the world. The same can be said for the reading of the Scriptures, or spiritual meditation, or any of the personal practices/disciplines.

---

[12]Clapp, *Tortured Wonders*, 88.

How, then, do we approach personal devotions given this perspective? First, as we have already argued, Christians should not engage in spiritual practices, whether they are individual or corporate, for the sole purpose of subjective, inward, emotional experience or sense of individual spiritual well-being. We engage in these "means of grace" for *formation* of the local body of Christ that includes us. This formation is the renewal of the image of God, in and through the life of the church, for the sake of the world. This understanding has the potential to radically change the way we understand and approach Christian spiritual practices. We may find it helpful to ask questions such as: Does this practice enhance the life of the body of Christ with which I am involved? Does this practice develop and enable the fruits of the Spirit to be embodied in the world? Is this practice ultimately about God and others or primarily about me? The core question is: What is the goal of this practice? If the goal is for the sake of the world (those inside and outside the church), then its impact on us and on the church becomes open to being supersized by extension into the lives of other Christians. If the goal of devotional practice is for me, then such isolated and self-focused practice will stagnate into something that is no more than experiential and remains puny with respect to its contribution to God's work in the world.

Second, consider the memorable passage of Scripture found in Hebrews 11–12. In Hebrews 11 the writer recounts a history of the all-stars of Christian faith. The writer begins with Abel, and works through Enoch, Noah, Abraham, Isaac, Jacob, Joseph, Moses, and Rahab. And just like any good writer/preacher, the author goes on to say that there's not enough time to talk about a bunch of other folks who have been tortured or put to death, or wandered in deserts and lived in holes, but the world was not worthy of them (Hebrews 11:35-38)! And then this: "These were all commended for their faith, yet none of them received what had been promised, since God had planned something better for us so that only together with us would they be made perfect" (Hebrews 11:39-40).

"Only together with us would they be made perfect." This is the reciprocal social extension of the gospel. We understand that even our perfection in Christ, our completion as individuals (what we would call in our Wesleyan tradition "sanctification"), takes place as a body, not as individuals.

Our perfection is completed as our Christian lives are enhanced by interactive and reciprocal extension into the life of the entire body of Christ. We are made perfect in one another. Because we are embodied persons, always embedded in situational contexts, capable of enhancement of capacities through cognitive extension, it takes the interactive body of Christ to form us into embodied Christians. Not only does it take a church to raise a Christian, it takes a holy church to form a holy person.

So, it makes sense to keep focused on the larger body when we read, "Therefore, since *we* are surrounded by such a great cloud of witnesses, let *us* throw off everything that hinders and the sin that so easily entangles. And let *us* run with perseverance the race marked out for *us*" (Hebrews 12:1, emphasis added). Because Christian life and thought is extended into this great cloud of witnesses, these all-stars of the faith, as well as our brothers and sisters in our local congregations, we should run this race together. How many times have we heard this passage preached in strongly individualistic ways? *You* should run the race, *you* should have perseverance, *you* should fix your eyes on Jesus. But if a life characterized by reciprocal cognitive extension within relational communities is truly what it means to be most fully human, with supersized cognitive and relational powers, then we should run together "the race marked out for us."

It is only through the body of Christ that we can live the Christian life in ways we might call supersized. When we try to do it alone, through individualized practices that focus on our private and internal states, or through seeking "awesome" subjective experiences (e.g., hiking in the woods or viewing a beautiful sunset), we will have had nothing more than an experience. Absent a wider extended and interactive life, the outcome will be an anemic kind of faith that does little to equip us to run the race together.

THE WIKIS OF
CHRISTIAN LIFE

IN CHAPTER FIVE WE INTRODUCED the idea of a "mental institution."[1] As understood in theories of extended cognition, a mental institution is a cognitive framework for understanding and acting in particular contexts which is the product of the accumulated experiences and thoughts of others. It is the preservation of the information and practices from the thinking and trial-and-error experiences of a multitude of individuals not currently present, but who have participated over time in the "building" of the mental institution. The example that we cited earlier was the legal system. In the next chapter we summarize Hutchins's analysis of the patterns of extended cognition in the navigation of a navy ship. In this context, he states that "we will not understand the computations [in navigation] until we follow its history back and see how structure has been accumulated over centuries"[2]—that is, appreciate the mental institutions that provide the structure for the navigational processes.

As an alternative to the term "mental institution," we suggest the more descriptive term "mental wiki." A wiki is a web-based resource (like Wikipedia) containing information on a particular subject that can be repeatedly and progressively modified and updated by a host of potential contributors—predominantly by individuals who know the topic well. There are two important aspects of a wiki as a metaphor that fulfill the idea of a mental institution and are critical to our discussion of cognitive extension: (1) wikis contain the accumulated and assembled contributions of a lot of other persons

---

[1]Shaun Gallagher, "The Socially Extended Mind," *Cognitive Systems Research* 25-26 (2013): 6.
[2]Edwin Hutchins, *Cognition in the Wild* (Cambridge, MA: MIT Press, 1995), 168.

over a period of time; and (2) as a webpage, a wiki contains knowledge that is readily available when needed to enhance our knowledge and thinking. Thus, a wiki is a medium that allows ready access to culturally accumulated information that can extend our cognitive capacities, but that does not require that we carry all the content around in our biological memories. It is ready-at-hand information—a quick search of a topic via our cellphone and we have before us a wiki of accumulated knowledge on the topic of interest.

Mental wikis are important in discussions of cognitive extension in that we can, when the context demands, incorporate the information and procedures to enhance our current thinking, planning, and problem solving—they supersize the mind. Our cognitive capacities are enhanced by mentally engaging networks of ideas and practices that are not the product of our own individual thought. In this chapter, we will consider the possibility for enhancement of Christian life by extension into networks of ideas and action possibilities that are not our own, and not always available from extensions to artifacts or other Christians in our immediate networks, but are given to us as uniquely Christian understandings, perspectives, and practices by the long and broad history of the Christian faith.

THE NATURE OF MENTAL WIKIS

Cultures (including religious traditions) involve a myriad of mental wikis. In fact, one could argue that culture is constituted by the sum total of the wikis that are deeply and inescapably embedded in our minds and in the implicit assumptions of our particular social world. As Merlin Donald writes, "Our cultures invade us and set our agendas."[3] We cannot escape the accumulation of knowledge, ideas, and semantic qualities of words that significantly scaffold our minds except perhaps via some intense countercultural experiences.

One good example of mental wikis that contribute to a culture is the accumulated knowledge about various forms of cooking. When cooking, we extend into prescribed procedures that we did not invent. To get beyond mere boiling water or microwaving an instant dinner, we need recipes derived from the experiences of other persons. Although a few things might be

---

[3]Merlin Donald, *A Mind So Rare: The Evolution of Human Consciousness* (New York: Norton, 2001), 298.

discovered by an isolated individual cook via trial and error, the usual method is to cognitively extend into the available wikis of a particular form of cooking. To become a gourmet cook would require a very deep extension into this form of wiki, including a choice as to which domain of cooking wiki one wishes to extend into—e.g., French, Mexican, Italian, Greek, Szechuan Chinese. Becoming an expert cook requires having available recipe books, cooking shows, YouTube videos, and/or cooking classes that allow a person access to the accumulated fund of knowledge of the particular culinary wiki. A gourmet cook is not necessarily one who invents a lot of new dishes but one who has become an expert in the ability to extend culinary thought and practice into the wiki of a particular form of cooking.

A mental wiki is more than simply a lot of individual bits of relevant information; it also involves schemas. Schemas are organized networks of important ideas that help us interact with and understand an entire complex situation or topic. In the cooking example above, one might have a general schema about what sorts of things go into French sauces, and what makes a tasty sauce versus a not-so-tasty sauce. Often schemas are story-like, involving sequences of actions and the outcomes that are likely to occur in these sorts of situations.

Another example of a schema would be deciding what to do when you encounter a person on the street who asks for money for gas for their car. What should you do? A person with a background of biblical stories might extend their thought into the story of the good Samaritan and, based on this story's action schema, give money to the person in apparent need. Alternatively, a schema/story might come to mind about persons using this plea as a scam to acquire money to buy drugs. Either way, mental processing with respect to what to do in this situation has been enhanced by extension into a schema or story that is not one's own creation but that comes to mind to enhance deliberation about what to do in this situation.

What we are calling wikis and schemas would include what Alasdair MacIntyre talks about as "practices" and "traditions." He writes, "By a 'practice' I . . . mean any coherent and complex form of socially established cooperative form of activity through which goods . . . are realized."[4] The wiki-like qualities

---

[4]Alasdair MacIntyre, *After Virtue*, 2nd ed. (Notre Dame: University of Notre Dame Press, 1981), 186

of practices include their dependence on history. MacIntyre states that "every practice has its own history. . . . To enter into a practice is to enter into a relationship not only with its contemporary practitioners, but also with those who have preceded us in the practice, particularly those whose achievements extended the reach of the practice to its present point."[5] However, MacIntyre warns that we should not presume that all practices (or all wikis) are necessarily good. "Some practices—that is, some coherent human activities which answer to the description of what I have called a practice—are evil."[6]

For MacIntyre, the wikis he calls "traditions" are larger patterns of thoughts and ideas that would encompass a group of related practices that together relate to the realization of a particular outcome (typically a good outcome). He writes, "For all reasoning takes place within the context of some traditional mode of thought. . . . Moreover, when a tradition is in good order it is always practically constituted by an argument about the goods the pursuit of which gives to that tradition its particular point and purpose."[7]

For example, an elementary school teacher will live her or his professional life within the tradition of elementary education providing a complex of practices that would, like wikis, be engaged to extend and enhance the cognitive processes of the teacher. Similarly, the various cultural and denominational manifestations of the Christian church constitute traditions with practices that can be engaged to extend and enhance the cognitive process of clergy and lay participants (for better or worse).

A large part of Christian life is accessing unique sorts of stories/schemas that we have learned that extend our decisions in particular situations. These schemas structure our thinking about how to act in ways that might never have come to mind outside of the capacity to extend into a narrative wiki about Christian life. It is important to note that accessing a mental wiki (and the information and schemas it contains) may not be conscious but rather provides implicit background knowledge to help successfully negotiate the situation.

Yet another way to think of mental wikis is as the cognitive-behavioral niches we described in chapter six. We pointed out, for example, that the definition

---

[5] Alasdair MacIntyre, *After Virtue*, 194,
[6] Alasdair MacIntyre, *After Virtue*, 199.
[7] Alasdair MacIntyre, *After Virtue*, 222.

of an organism should include the environmental niche that it occupies—as in a spider and its web. The web is an essential part (an extension) of the spider's adaptive intelligent behavior. A mental wiki is for human beings analogous to the spider's web. Behavior that involves a wiki/niche can be seen as manifesting hybrid agency—the cause of the behavior is both the organism and its niche. Similarly, the living of a Christian life is a form of hybrid agency consisting of the person, the church within which the person was and is formed, and the Christian wikis available to enhance thinking, deciding, and acting.

At this point we must make note of an important caveat about mental wikis (schemas/niches). These systems of understanding that influence our thought and behavior may be adaptive or maladaptive. For example, an organized-crime family would constitute a system of influences (a niche) involving mental wikis for members, however unhealthy the influences might be. What makes something a mental wiki is an accumulation and assemblage of information, structures, and processes, but the specific *content* may be of most any sort. Thus, these aids to thought and behavior are networks of ideas and mental processes that hold influences that can be good or bad, healthy or unhealthy, caring or merciless, violent or nonviolent, Christian, pseudo-Christian, or non-Christian.

Another important characteristic is that a wiki, schema, or niche typically does not function like a set of rigid rules or an inflexible instruction manual. Wikis differ on how much or how little direction or specific information they offer persons or groups who enter into them. Think about the difference between the performance of classical orchestral music compared to that of a jazz quartet that specializes in improvisation. Jazz may sound like "anything goes," but experienced jazz players know that there is an accepted and established form and method (wiki) to the improvisational madness. One of the things that makes improvisational jazz so exciting even for the uninitiated is how at one moment it seems so boundlessly chaotic, only to have it coalesce together in the next. Most of the wikis that inform our daily lives are more like the general schemas that coordinate jazz improvisation than a more tightly constrained orchestral performance.[8]

---

[8]Thanks to IVP editor Jon Boyd, a jazz player, for bringing this example to us.

Nevertheless, like the ongoing progression of amendments to most Wikipedia entries, our contributions to "wikiness" are more like tweaks than major alterations. As Merlin Donald puts it,

> It is a rare idea, thought, hypothesis, or archetype that has not already been conceived and modified a thousand times, somewhere in the distributed webs of the human cognitive universe. The best an individual can hope for is a small degree of uniqueness, perhaps by becoming the conduit of new collisions of ideas or conjoining vectors of thoughts that have never before been brought together.[9]

WIKIS OF CHRISTIAN LIFE

Given the descriptions above, it should not be too much of a stretch to think of Christian life as extended by a rich and robust set of wikis involving the historically accumulated body of practices and traditions of the church. Biblical stories and teachings form the core of the mental wikis of Christian life. In addition, many of the practices of Christian life are rooted in the history of thinking, creativity, and actions of many who have participated in the life of the church in previous times, either recent or historical. For example, in worship we enter into practices through which our minds are extended into an ecclesial mental institution with a very long history (although perhaps modified in the current context to create a sense of freshness). As we dynamically and creatively soft couple into the institution of worship, we access mental and behavioral structures that are not of our own invention, yet serve to significantly extend and enhance our thoughts, imaginations, and practices.

Remember the story about Otto and the notebook that he uses to supersize a memory that is seriously weakened by Alzheimer's disease. Philosophers who use this story to discuss issues of extended cognition talk of the critical issue of *belief*.[10] That is, it is not just that Otto has information written in the notebook but also that Otto believes that the information in the notebook is true. The notebook is an element that enhances his memory because of this belief, just as persons with normal memories believe that what comes to their minds, via the processes of their brain, is a true memory of some past event.

[9]Donald, *A Mind So Rare*, 299.
[10]Andy Clark, *Supersizing the Mind: Embodiment, Action, and Cognitive Extension* (Oxford, UK: Oxford University Press, 2011).

This is not unlike our problem as Christians in believing what we cannot see or experience directly. The wikis of Christian faith (including biblical stories, theological creeds, liturgies, and rituals) not only hold what needs to be remembered, but are credited as true, and thus are experienced as enhancements of Christian life. Our Christian faith is belief in wikis we have received.

The idea of a Christian life that is nested within mental wikis raises again the question of the degree to which we can consider our Christian lives as uniquely our own, or whether we are, in fact, engaging in practices and accessing perspectives given to us by the church. As we engage in thoughts, activities, conversations, worship, prayers, etc., we are often tempted to consider these to be manifestations of our own individual spirituality. However, are we not recapitulating the thoughts and practices of other Christians as these have been taught to us by the church (though often tweaked to meet the current context)? Similarly, as we argued in chapter seven, much as we might tend to consider individual activities such as personal devotional practices to be aspects of our own unique spirituality, they are in reality extensions into the mental wikis made available to us by the church and a very long history of Christian thought and life.

Important Christian mental wikis would include theology and doctrines, rites and rituals, forms of worship, individual spiritual disciplines, Christian ethics, and schemas of compassionate actions, as well as ideas about Christian engagement in secular things like occupations, recreation, economics, politics, and family life. Accessing these wikis to regulate our daily thoughts and behaviors, or to solve immediate problems, involves cognitive extension into the minds of a host of other persons who, over time, built and molded the frameworks available to us as Christians. Our agency as Christians is always a hybrid of ourselves and the mental institutions (wikis, systems, niches) that we occupy.[11]

One of the important aspects of mental wikis is the degree to which they provide us with a constructive learning system. That is, our network of understanding around a particular situation or topic (the relevant mental wiki)

---

[11]As we have mentioned before, what we are describing in this book is an understanding of the immanent aspect of our Christian lives—the presence and accessibility of God in this present physical world. We also recognize and value the possibility of the unprecedented moving of the Spirit of God within groups or within individual persons.

provides the prerequisite basic mental and behavioral structures that can allow us to assimilate further information, ideas, and potential actions related to this domain. Dwelling in the mental institution of cooking allows one to readily learn and assimilate new cooking ideas and processes, while some of these ideas are beyond the understanding of persons not deeply nested in the mental wikis of cooking. Similarly, the Christian formation of individuals is progressive in that, as we actively access the mental wikis of the Christian faith, we also gain a constructive learning system for deeper understanding of Christian life and faith.[12] And just like improvisational jazz, a Christian wiki may have different degrees of freedom in terms of how much improvisation is allowed. Some Christian traditions are known for the clear boundaries and restrictions they put on persons who live within them, while others are known for being wider and wilder in the breadth of their specifications and expectations.

Again, we offer the cautionary note that the mental wikis of a particular group or church can either hold what is truly Christian or can institutionalize what is not truly Christian. Since mental wikis are often implicit and unconsciously accessed, it is difficult to examine the truth of the wikis into which we cognitively extend. Long-standing practices and assumptions are often too hidden from consciousness to be mindfully evaluated. It is also possible to unconsciously blend two or more wikis into one. An important example can be found in some versions of Western evangelicalism in the form of a syncretistic blending of the secular wiki of nationalism (and all that comes along with that idea) with the ideas (wikis) that surround biblical teaching regarding the kingdom of God.

RITES AND RITUALS AS WIKIS

There is a tendency for some religious people to view participation in the rites and rituals of their faith as magical. That is, they view participation in the ritual as magically changing the person, transforming them to a new religious state. For example, some Christian views of Eucharist and baptism have this flavor. An alternative view of rites and rituals is that they are behavioral cues to critical mental wikis of the particular faith. They are embodied reminders of the content of core religious wikis that enhance understanding of the faith.

---

[12]We recognize that ongoing formation and growth does not typify some Christians. Our task here is to describe the nature and possibilities of formation, not to account for the reasons it may not occur.

For example, Eucharist serves as a reminder and reenactment of the story of the Last Supper. In addition, it carries a whole network of associations and reminders of core ideas in Christian faith—ideas like Jesus' crucifixion and sacrifice (the body and blood of Christ), meal and fellowship, and the commission to the church to love one another. Each of these ideas involve large and complex networks of particular thoughts, associations, and schemas about the nature of our faith that are elicited as we participate in the Eucharist. Much the same sort of thing can be said about baptism. This Christian rite is a signal to mental wikis involving ideas such as cleansing from sin, death and resurrection, and birth and new life, as well as having connotations of initiation and membership. Although Eucharist and baptism are the most notable examples, much of worship is formed around signals and cues to the mental wikis of Christian faith. Eucharist, baptism, and the other Christian rituals, rites, and observances provide important scaffolding for the cognitive niche within which Christian life is lived. Rather than magic, these rituals and rites form us by a natural embodied learning process which occurs as we participate in embodied, metaphorically meaningful actions.

LANGUAGE AND CHRISTIAN WIKIS

Language forms an important part of mental wikis. Due to the fact that words codify and summarize complex ideas, language often points to particular wikis. It is not simply the words that we use or how we use them but also what we understand a word to mean and the complex of associations that a word triggers in our minds. Consider the word *gay*. A century ago this word denoted something very different than it does in modern parlance. It is not just the denotative meaning that has changed but also the nuances of semantic associations surrounding the word that vary remarkably within different cultural groups and their respective mental institutions.

The impact of language on thought functions at different levels. At the lowest level, words create perceptions and attention to things that would otherwise escape notice. A word like *compassion* gathers certain experiences into a category of similar events, after which the word allows us to perceive and attend to the quality of compassion in human interactions. At a higher level, language guides action by allowing us to think about past actions and possibilities for future action. To say "we must act compassionately" engenders and sustains actions of a particular kind which we would not be able to imagine for ourselves or for others without the tool of language. At the highest level, language is a critical part of mental wikis. What has been constructed over time by the many individuals who contributed to a particular mental wiki exists mostly in language—in context-specific nuances of meaning and in language-coded processes of thought and action. At times a single word, such as *sanctification*, can contain a whole universe of meanings and actions.

Much of the Christian life that we inherit is constructed and available to us in the particular meanings of words and the behaviors and interactions that the words imply. Consider the Christian nuances around words like *sacrifice*, *love*, *community*, *testimony*, and *sin*. Christian faith, belief, and life are expressed in ways that involve uniquely nuanced and corporately constructed meanings. While prayer can include nonverbal meditative states and experiences, its primary realization is expressed in words— words that draw on unique meanings and the broad range of concepts in the wikis of Christian life. As we described previously (chapters six and seven), we pray with words whose particular meanings we did not invent and with reference to ideas we did not create. Thus, Christian life is supersized as our minds are extended by the language created and shared in the Christian community.

A critical role of language in cognitive extension is as the medium for storytelling. The obvious example is the biblical stories that form the core of Christian life. But there are also narratives shared between Christians in community (for example, testimonies)—narratives of God's blessing, or of acts of compassion and mercy within the community, or of life gone awry but redeemed by God through the church. In both cases (biblical and congregational), the narratives told within Christian congregations—in preaching, teaching, testimony, Bible study, and prayer—are incorporated by extension in ways that enhance our imaginations regarding the nature of Christian life. The wikis of Christian life are dominated by narratives.

As we described in chapter seven, a critical factor in the power of stories is that, in order to understand the actions in the story, the hearer must create in their imagination a simulation of the actions and interactions described in the narrative.[13] To say within a story "he climbed the mountain" is to cause to occur within the hearer's brain systems a quick partial simulation (a mental thumbnail action sketch) of climbing a mountain. Otherwise the hearer cannot adequately appreciate what is being said. Recent brain research has shown activation of the same brain areas in a listener that would be activated if the listener were doing the actions being described in a story.[14] Thus, the hearer mentally extends into the events being described in the story by brain-based action simulation. What is more, behavioral simulations leave residues in neural pathways that increase (however subtly) the likelihood of the hearer doing the action described in the story—particularly if the action described is evaluated as effective and good by the hearer. Our action tendencies as Christians are formed in us by stories of Christian life into which we extend ourselves via action simulation.

Stories do not exist in isolation from the larger network of ideas, schemas, systems, and behavioral niches that form the mental wikis of our Christian lives. The wikis that we inhabit influence our theological interpretations of both biblical and community stories. Any story can be followed by the question, "So what?" The mental wikis of Christian life and faith provide the interpretive theological and practical framework that answers this question. As Lesslie Newbigin has said, "The only hermeneutic of the gospel is a congregation of men and women who believe it and live by it."[15] Our congregational lives hold and progressively tweak to meet our context, the mental wikis within which we understand the gospel.

However, as we have tried to make clear, these broader mental institutions—our everyday wikis of Christian life—may or may not be truly Christian. Thus, the nature of these (typically implicit) ideas, schemas, systems, and niches that provide the context and scaffolding around congregational and individual lives should always be open to examination. We need to be mindful of the mental wikis that we inhabit and the degree to which they have become dominated by the powerful wikis of the broader cultural world we occupy.

---

[13]Christian Keysers, *The Empathic Brain: How the Discovery of Mirror Neurons Changes Our Understanding of Human Nature* (self-pub., Amazon Digital Services, 2011), Kindle, 107-8.

[14]Annabel D. Nijhof and Roel M. Willems, "Simulating Fiction: Individual Differences in Literature Comprehension Revealed with FMRI," *PLoS One* 10, no. 2 (2015): e0116492, https://doi.org/10.1371/journal.pone.0116492.

[15]Lesslie Newbigin, *The Gospel in a Pluralist Society* (Grand Rapids: Eerdmans, 1989), 227.

NARRATIVE CHRISTIAN IDENTITY

The role and importance of story-based wikis go deeper than simply structuring particular domains of actions or understandings. Psychologist Dan McAdams and others have argued that we hold our self-identity in narrative form.[16] We understand ourselves as central characters in an unfolding drama. We adopt a story (or stories) about ourselves that gives our lives meaning and coherence. However, the stories we would tell about ourselves are not entirely our own but are narrative structures that we borrow or are given to us. We find our identity narratives in stories from family, mentors, heroes of books or movies, sports idols, etc. The self-identity narratives that we adopt are part of the cultural wikis that we inherit and that are available for extending our imaginations about ourselves.

Similarly, our identity as Christians is formed by inhabiting particular stories. Some of the stories come to us in themes from biblical narratives, but more often they come in the narratives we assimilate from our church and the lives of other Christians. The stories help us give Christian meaning to our past and present, but they also feed our imagination regarding the future and guide the unfolding of our Christian lives. Frequently others help us narrate our own stories by telling us about ourselves. We are the stories we use to narrate our lives and the stories others tell us about ourselves. And these stories we do not invent but are part of the mental wikis given to us that we extend into that form and enhance our thinking about Christian life.

This book is about a new understanding of Christian life that includes what is beyond our individual selves. In this chapter we have considered what is available as opportunities for the extension and enhancement of Christian life by cognitive extension into what we have called "wikis"—that is, information, practices, schemas, niches, and stories that we did not create but that can supersize our Christian lives. It is not simply that these mental wikis have some direct effect on us as isolated individuals but also that these wikis are the niches within which we exist and into which we can extend our thoughts and imaginations in order to live a richer and more robust Christian life. "We are a culturally bound species and live in a symbiosis with our collective creation."[17]

---

[16]Dan McAdams, *The Redemptive Self: Stories Americans Live By* (New York: Oxford University Press, 2005).
[17]Donald, *A Mind So Rare*, 300.

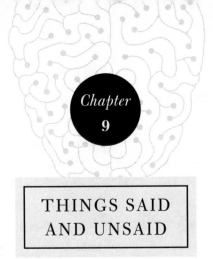

THINGS SAID
AND UNSAID

AS WE NEAR THE END OF THIS BOOK we wish to deal with two issues or concerns that we suspect readers may have had while reading. First is our somewhat idealistic view of the church as compared to the churches that exist in many communities. Where do you find such a church? Or how do you become such a church? The second issue is the strong theology of the immanence of God that clearly characterizes the arguments of this book. Whatever happened to the transcendence of God?

WHERE DO YOU FIND THIS CHURCH?

Internet technology guru Clay Shirky, in his book *Cognitive Surplus: Creativity and Generosity in a Connected Age,* tells the following story:

> I was having dinner with a group of friends, talking about our kids, and one of them told a story about watching a DVD with his four-year-old daughter. In the middle of the movie, apropos of nothing, she jumped up off the couch and ran around behind the screen. My friend thought she wanted to see if the people in the movie were really back there. But that wasn't what she was up to. She started rooting around in the cables behind the screen. Her dad asked, "What are you doing?" And she stuck her head out from behind the screen and said, "Looking for the mouse."[1]

This little girl had already assimilated the idea that the media she encounters are things she interacts with, not something she watches passively. Anything

---

[1] Clay Shirky, *Cognitive Surplus: Creativity and Generosity in a Connected Age* (New York: Penguin Press, 2010), 212.

with a screen must have a mouse to allow interactions. She was not willing to sit still and merely watch.

Shirky comments that "media that's targeted at you but doesn't include you may not be worth sitting still for."[2] What follows considers questions such as, What sort of church is worth sitting still for? If Christian life is supersized by networks of interactive soft coupling among the ecclesia, what sort of group welcomes this? Where do you find the mouse (the interactive plug points) in the life of this church?

We have been arguing that vital Christian life is not possible in isolation but that a richer and more robust (supersized) life is possible by extension of that life into groups, congregations, churches, and traditions. In making this argument, we have assumed a somewhat ideal church—a church that fosters extension and has genuine plug points for interactive soft coupling into the life of the church. We have assumed a church where you can readily find the mouse. Making this assumption is, of course, to view the church through rose-colored glasses, presuming characteristics that may or may not be present in any particular church.

Shirky talks about "The People Formerly Known as the Audience" who have now become participants.[3] The move from TV watching to online computer interactions increasingly conditions people to be less tolerant of entertainment and information that is not interactive. In a connected age people are no longer willing to be passive recipients of information targeted *at them* but are looking for sources that *include them* as interactive participants. They are looking for the mouse—the point of interactivity. They are looking for opportunities to participate and create. What is necessary for vital extension into groups and systems is interactivity and generativity—creative action and feedback, behavior and response, idea and new idea, prayer and prayer response, teaching and pushback. One might say that today the issue is not church attendance or membership but church engagement.

In considering the nature of churches with respect to the possibility that an individual might extend their Christian life into the life of a particular church, two questions are important to consider: (1) the basic human desires

---

[2]Shirky, *Cognitive Surplus*, 212.
[3]Shirky, *Cognitive Surplus*, 64.

that might motivate extension and participation, and (2) the openness of the systems and culture of the church to more than passive attendance.

In everything people do, motivations are critical to what they do and how they do it. Clay Shirky describes four important human motivations that serve to draw people into volunteer engagement with groups and projects: the intrinsic motives of autonomy and competency and the social motives of connectedness and sharing.[4]

Autonomy. This seems like a contradiction with respect to ideas of becoming plugged in and interconnected. However, what is meant here is the degree to which a person feels as if their presence can contribute in some *particular* way. They are hoping not to be simply an addition to the count in the audience size. People are more apt to plug in where they see that they have a contribution to make to the whole. They are also looking for an opportunity to work in a way that is in some respect self-supervised. They wish to contribute in a way that feels like what they do expresses something about them and contributes to the larger whole.

Competency. It is not just the sense of autonomy that motivates people, but it is the sense that they can plug in in a way that draws on, and allows them to express, some form of competency—that they have a way to use their skills and life experiences to enhance the life of the church and others in the church. However, what is meant by competence is not professional-level skill but opportunity to express whatever form of competence one has in a way that contributes. In open-source projects (discussed below) the whole point is what can be accomplished with the contributions of amateurs.

Connectedness. Audiences do not connect, participants do. The connection that is desired is not the en masse emotional experiences of a rock concert or the sentimental social interactions of chitchat at a party. In a connected age, people are more than ever looking for situations (churches) where they can find the mouse that connects them into a larger interactive project as an autonomous and competent participant—the interactive connectivity of participation in significant work. Connecting to the plug points of interactive projects allows for the simultaneous experiences of "I did it! We did it!"[5]

---

[4]Shirky, *Cognitive Surplus*, 74-82.
[5]Shirky, *Cognitive Surplus*, 79.

Sharing. It is also true of human nature that the opportunity to connect in a way that expresses autonomy and competency is motivated most heartily when it includes the opportunity to share—to give generously to the benefit of others through what one is able to do. People are implicitly motivated and rewarded by opportunities to do something that results in a benefit to others. The best work is always done for the love of the work itself and as an expression of love for others.

The second issue to consider with respect to whether a particular church provides opportunity for the sort of extension that supersizes Christian life is whether the culture of the church—its systems, procedures, and implicit presuppositions—is genuinely open to allowing people to plug in in ways that meet these motivations. Behavior follows opportunity, so the question is, Where are the opportunities for satisfying motives of autonomy, competence, connectedness, and sharing?

An enlightening domain in which to think about this question is the relationship between corporate and open-source software production. Clay Shirky writes and talks a lot about the comparison between commercial software projects like Microsoft Windows or Apple iOS and open-source projects like the Unix operating system. Commercial production of software by corporations is entirely in-house work done by small teams of closely managed and controlled software professionals. The open-source software development method is public, open to all, and collaborative. It allows anyone who wishes to contribute to make changes and improvements to the software (as long as they abide by the minimal rules of participation). The Unix operating system has developed over time by the contributions of thousands of volunteer programmers (mostly amateurs) who participated primarily because of motivations like autonomy, competency, connectedness, and sharing. In open-source development, quality is "managed" by self-corrective processes in the ongoing interactions of editing and improvements done by the very large number of participants. Also, a participant can make large and many contributions, or a few small contributions, but the numerous small contributions cannot be undervalued in the ongoing improvements of the software.

Some of the contrasts between the commercial and open-source modes of software development are: professional versus amateur contributors, paid versus volunteer work, extrinsic (money) versus intrinsic (love of the work) motivations, prespecified work versus the freedom and joy of experimentation, and corporate profit versus the chance to generously share one's work with others for free. Shirky comments on the "ability of loosely coordinated groups with a shared culture to perform tasks more effectively than individuals, more effectively than markets using price signals, and more effectively than governments using managerial direction."[6]

In thinking about extended Christian life, and participant churches with plug points where congregants can find the mouse, the open-source model is worth considering. Does a particular church look more like a corporate, highly managed, professionally implemented project? Or is the life of the church open-source, where congregants are free to contribute in any aspect of the life of the congregation? Are the plug points—the opportunities for engagement—obvious? Can those who attend—persons who otherwise live in an interactive and participatory online world—find the interaction points, or are they stuck at church looking for the mouse? The modern interactive world seems to require the church to become more open-source, avoiding the commercial mode of professionals only, highly skilled only, or clergy only.

There are issues to consider in an open-source mode where the implications differ between software development and congregational environments. Group size is critical and interacts with the medium of interaction. A very large group was able to participate in the Unix project because everything happened online. The church operates face-to-face and in real time, therefore the size of the group of participants will need to be smaller. The costs of participating are also different. The web provides easy, low-cost interactions between large groups, while the church mostly operates within the higher social costs implied again by face-to-face and real-time interaction. Clarity of mission is also a critical factor. The mission is quite specific, clear, and relatively constrained in software development. In the church, mission is often less specific and clear, and typically very broad, and thus requires constant restating and refocusing. A final critical element in an open-source environment is its culture—the implicit assumptions about how the group should

---

[6]Shirky, *Cognitive Surplus*, 128.

go about its work. Open-source software projects operate by rather clear assumptions and guidelines for participation. Churches vary widely in this regard. To take advantage of the power of an open-source mode in a church, attention must be paid to the church's culture.

In all, it seems that the church has much to gain by reducing reliance on a top-down, hierarchical, and centrally managed understanding of local church life and adopting the power of open-source modes for the life and work of a congregation.

WHATEVER HAPPENED TO TRANSCENDENCE?

To the degree that our discussions in this book qualify as theology, it is theological anthropology and ecclesiology that is our focus. We are interested in the nature of human beings as they relate to the reign of God on earth, and most particularly to the life of the church. Our discussions of the nature of Christian life, formation, the church, worship, and devotional life are all focused on understanding these domains from the point of view of the cognitive and psychosocial nature of persons. Therefore, the particular quality of the work and reign of God in the world that is represented in this sort of discussion is God's *immanence*. That is to say, we are interested in the ways God is manifest within the created world—most particularly in the nature of created persons and human interactivity in the life of the church. Part of what motivates this project is a suspicion that the immanence of God in human interactions is easily ignored or downplayed by in-the-pews theology. Attending to or ignoring the immanent work of God in the interactivity of human life has consequences. As theologian Mildred Bangs Wynkoop has written, "What one believes about human nature and God's grace, then, will have a direct bearing on the kind of Christian life one experiences."[7]

No human discussion or discourse can ever do justice to the entirety of God. In this respect we realize that in this book we have left unsaid a great deal about the transcendent activity of God in the world. We have said little about the wholly independent work of God in his creation and particularly in the lives of Christians and the church. It is not that we don't believe in the

---

[7]Mildred Bangs Wynkoop, *Foundations of Wesleyan-Arminian Theology*, (Kansas City, MO: Beacon Hill Press, 1967), 109.

transcendent activity of God in the world. However, the points that we wish to help our readers better understand are about the nature of the immanent work of God within the physical, cognitive, and social lives of human beings. The concept of cognitive extension and the supersizing of Christian life is about how God through the Spirit operates within the interactive lives of Christians and in the lives of churches and congregations.

We confess that we are drawn to consideration of God's immanent work in the affairs of human life for two important reasons. First, we are both psychologists—Brad a clinical psychologist and Warren an experimental neuropsychologist. Our expertise in areas of psychology leads us to focus on the dynamics of human life, including the phenomena surrounding extended cognition and its implications for Christian life. We are deeply interested in the intersection of how being human impacts Christian faith and practice. Second, we are both theologically Wesleyan. As such we naturally tend to think about the dynamics of human freedom: actions, choices, and responsibilities.

When groups hear us present on embodied, embedded, and extended cognition and Christian life, someone inevitably asks, "Where is the Holy Spirit?" We usually assume that they are implying more than they are explicitly asking. They usually are implying that our model sounds too humanist, reductionist, or materialist—as if somehow all of these processes are happening outside of God's grace and activity and that we are falling into a kind of Pelagian approach to Christianity (i.e., a righteousness based on works).

We have come to understand that this question can only be answered from a particular theological position or tradition.[8] This is because different Christian traditions have different ways of understanding the role of the Holy Spirit in human life and the consequent relationship between divine intervention and human responsibility. For example, persons who hear us lecture (or read our previous book) and ask, "Where is the Holy Spirit?" are often operating from a Christian tradition that emphasizes the inherent sinfulness

---

[8]For discussions about the importance of theological traditions on the dialogue between psychology and theology, see Steven J. Sandage and Jeannine K. Brown, *Relational Integration of Psychology and Christian Theology: Theory, Research, and Practice* (New York: Routledge, 2018); Brad D. Strawn, Ron Wright, and Paul Jones, "Tradition-Based Integration: Illuminating the Stories and Practices That Shape Our Integrative Imaginations," *Journal of Psychology & Christianity* 33, no. 4 (2014): 300-310; and Ron Wright, Paul Jones, and Brad Strawn, "Tradition-Based Integration," in *Christianity & Psychoanalysis: A New Conversation*, eds. Earl D. Bland and Brad D. Strawn (Downers Grove, IL: InterVarsity Press, 2014), 37-54.

of human nature and our inability to accomplish anything apart from a super-natural in-breaking of the Spirit. This kind of "supernatural theism"[9] often leads Christians to use language of the Spirit that is not found in the New Testament, such as "surrender to" or "possessed by," instead of the actual language used in the New Testament, "filled with."[10] So rather than the Spirit being something coming from outside the human experience that humans must "surrender to," perhaps the Spirit "fills" the human experience, especially those experiences in which persons extend their lives into the lives of one another.

It is therefore the Spirit, God himself, who continues the ongoing work of sanctification in the life of the believer, and from the Wesleyan tradition, this points toward the development and attainment of the fruits of the Spirit. Furthermore, this does not mean a suppression by the Spirit of human nature or creation, although creation must be dedicated, cleansed, and disciplined. God in Christ Jesus and through the Spirit redeems creation, awakens the human moral nature, and invites participation of the human in the eschatological work of making all things new. This divine-human interaction is a kind of reciprocating renewal, a kind of "thirdness"[11] in which the Spirit emerges. This is never forced upon the person but is in fact a kind of "responsible grace"[12] in which humans can fully participate with God in processes located within the means of creation that God has put in place from the very beginning. We see and understand the processes that humans can participate in and with God as a kind of "immanental cosmology"[13] at the very heart of creation. While we are not attempting to convert the reader to any particular theological tradition, we have tried to explain our approach in hopes that the reader will find ways to think about these ideas in light of their own theological tradition.

---

[9]Marcus Borg, *The God We Never Knew: Beyond Dogmatic Religion to a More Authentic Contemporary Faith* (San Francisco: HarperCollins, 2009), 12

[10]Wynkoop, *Foundations of Wesleyan-Arminian Theology*, 111.

[11]For a complex theological, psychotherapeutic, and psychoanalytic understanding of thirdness and the Spirit, see Marie T. Hoffman, *Toward Mutual Recognition: Relational Psychoanalysis and the Christian Narrative* (New York: Routledge, 2011).

[12]See Randy L. Maddox, *Responsible Grace: John Wesley's Practical Theology* (Nashville: Kingswood Books, 1994) for an in-depth look at Wesleyan theology and particularly the divine-human interaction.

[13]Michael Lodahl, "The Cosmological Basis for John Wesley's 'Gradualism,'" *Wesleyan Theological Journal* 32, no. 1 (1997): 17-32.

This brings us back to ideas about ways in which a Christian life is supersized by extension of life into a congregational context—a context that is, in one sense, very human, but also capable of collectively embodying the immanent work of God. We believe that the Spirit of God is (can be, should be) particularly manifest in the interactive space between Christians and within congregations. It is this collective embodiment and extension between believers (i.e., the church) which informs our understanding of the Wesleyan idea of being "filled with the Spirit." However incomplete our analysis may be, we believe this discussion of extended cognition and Christian life provides some basis for understanding Matthew 18:20: "For where two or three gather in my name, there am I with them."

METAPHORS OF A
NEW PARADIGM

THE IDEAS ABOUT CHRISTIAN LIFE that we have discussed in this book are novel and not intuitively obvious, particularly to us who have been enculturated into a strongly individualistic way of thinking about Christian life. This is not the way we have been taught to understand ourselves, our bodies, or our relationship to the body of persons that is the church. The idea of a Christian life that is extended beyond the self is a paradigm shift.

Within this new paradigm, an important implication is that mental processes are *inherently* extended (always operative in mental processing) and not simply *secondarily* extended (an added enhancement when otherwise a problem can't be solved). As we have described, although extension is dynamic, changing in its configuration from moment to moment, it should not be understood as "in addition to" whatever goes on in the brain but as an integral part of human mental processing. When mental processes seem to be done within the brain/body systems of a single individual, these processes are based upon simulations of previously experienced interactions with environmental artifacts, other persons, and/or information derived from sources outside the self (mental wikis). Thus, thinking is always extended beyond the person in some way. Although much was learned within the previous model of the human mind (that is, the information processing model rooted in the brain-as-computer analogy), the broader context is being reshaped in a way that changes what we think about "thinking," and ultimately our views of human life.

Similarly, part of this paradigm shift is the realization that Christian life as extended does not imply simply a helpful add-on to whatever goes on inside the individual person—something that would be nice to incorporate but is not essential. Rather, we are arguing that Christian life (and what we think of as "spirituality") is inherently and inescapably extended into people and processes that are outside of ourselves. Christian life cannot be thought of as existing in a vacuum that does not include what is happening in the space between the person and the life of the people of God. Extended Christian living is not an outward sign of some inward state but *is* the thing designated by a person's "Christian faith" or "spirituality."

Implied by the framework we are advocating is also a shift in our understanding of the goal of a Christian life. If the goal is the salvation of individual persons, then the primary target is something unique and specific to each individual person. If the goal is about the people of God and the reign of God, then the target is not first and foremost about individual persons. It is about the network of reciprocal extension that forms the body of Christ. Such a network is significant both as a corporate sign of God's presence and as an arm of God's work in the world.

Much of what we have been considering has been framed in the context of enhancing (supersizing) the Christian life of individuals. However, as soon as we widen our view a bit, we see that this inescapably involves the wider network of reciprocal extensions within a congregation and brings into focus the question of the ultimate goal of any supersizing. The primary goal is the vitality of the life and work of the body of Christ, not individual spiritual status. Therefore, as far as an individual is concerned, their goal is something like, "What is it that the particular body of Christ that I am a part of needs from me for it to participate with God's work in this body of believers and local community?"[1] And as we have described, such engagement with a community of believers has the reciprocal added value of enhancing the ongoing formation of the Christian lives of the persons involved.

NAVIGATING A LARGE SHIP

An illustration of extended cognition from another domain might facilitate shifting our paradigm for thinking about Christian life and the church. Edwin

---

[1] The thinking that gives rise to this question is related to the discussion of virtue by Alasdair MacIntyre in *After Virtue*.

Hutchins, in his book *Cognition in the Wild*, illustrates cognitive extension and the characteristics of an interactive network of extension as it occurs in the navigation of a large naval ship.[2] We offer this illustration to demonstrate specific examples of cognitive extension and how they operate together to accomplish a highly complex collaborative task, and as a *conceptual metaphor*[3] of the church (more of this latter point later).

Hutchins describes the complex processes and procedures that take place on the bridge that are necessary to successfully navigate a large navy ship. He describes in great detail the highly complex and dynamic network of forms of cognitive extensions that results in accurate navigation. These extensions involve instruments and interpersonal interactions that come together to accomplish a task that is not within the capacities of a single person. He also describes how this entire process is framed and guided by the wikis of centuries of accumulated knowledge about the processes of successful navigation of a boat at sea. In a well-orchestrated series of operations involving a number of different individuals, each operating with different tools, the immediate position and trajectory of the ship is determined, and decisions are made about any changes necessary to guide the ship toward its destination.

For example, Hutchins describes a number of tools that enhance the process of fixing the position of the ship. One is called an *alidade*, which is a telescope-like instrument that the operator aligns with a point on land, then reads the compass direction to the object and its angle with respect to the center axis of the ship. This information is fed to the persons working with the chart. Without this tool of observational extension, the relationship of the ship to the landmark could only be represented in a way not precise enough for accurate navigation. The extended mental processing allowed by the alidade enables this particular crew member to contribute something critical to the ongoing process of navigation.

Another set of tools that extend the cognitive process of navigation are the charts available. Large naval ships carry in the neighborhood of five thousand

---

[2] Edwin Hutchins, *Cognition in the Wild* (Cambridge, MA: MIT Press, 1995).
[3] Modern linguistics has advanced the idea of a "conceptual metaphor," which is different from the prior idea of a metaphoric word or phrase (referred to as an "image metaphor") in that it serves to map a large body of knowledge onto the domain to be illustrated and understood. For more on this, see George Lakoff, "Conceptual Metaphor," in *Cognitive Linguistics: Basic Readings*, ed. Dirk Geeraerts (Berlin, Germany: Mouton de Gruyter, 2006), 189-96.

different charts. Each chart contains a large amount of information about shorelines, water depths, hazards, configurations of ports, etc. that could not be reasonably assembled within the lifetime of any one navigator or group of navigators. The chart information significantly extends and enhances the cognitive processes of navigation. On the currently relevant chart, a tool called a *hoey* (a protractor-like device) is used to construct lines from the information about the relative position of various landmarks from the alidade sightings. These lines will intersect on the chart at the exact position of the ship. The hoey extends cognition by embodying mathematical calculations into the instrument itself so that they do not have to be done at the moment by the navigator. The alidade, charts, and hoey are only a few of the complex set of tools available that extend and enhance the cognitive processes of navigation.

Successful navigation also involves the interactions of many individuals, each in some way extending the cognitive processing of other individuals, and thus enhancing the work of the group as a whole. In this manner the eventual decision-making processes of the captain are robustly enhanced by being extended into the processes of the entire bridge. This interactive network of persons that accomplish the navigation generally includes about ten persons, such as a navigator, assistant navigator, navigation plotter and time recorder, port and starboard alidade operators, Fathometer operator, and the quartermaster of the watch who serves as helmsman. Each has different roles, different abilities, and at any moment, a different part of the critical information. These all have to couple their work and knowledge into a smoothly functioning interactive network in order to fix an updated position and make navigational adjustments, in some cases every three minutes.

Thus, various individuals know how to do different processes or how to correctly use various specific tools. The critical outcome of accurate navigation is a property that emerges not from individual knowledge, or observational processes, or calculations, but from the interactive work of the entire group. For the process of successful navigation, what is inside the head of any particular participant (in terms of depth of general knowledge about navigation or other aspects of seamanship) is not critically important so long as each person executes their particular process in a timely and accurate manner to contribute to guiding the ship safely forward toward its destination. As

Merlin Donald puts it in his discussion of the collectivity of mind, "We do our most important intellectual work as connected members of cultural networks. . . . Single individuals rarely play an indispensable role."[4]

It is also important to keep in mind that the ultimate level of concern is the entire ship, not individual persons, although each individual has an important role to play. The marker of success is accurate and safe ship navigation, not something about the work of individual sailors. And the bridge and its navigational processes is only one of many systems serving in the work and life of the ship that must function well for the ship to fulfill its intended mission.

DESIGNING SPACESHIPS

We began this book with a story of "hidden figures"—the African American women mathematicians involved in the engineering of the first rockets and space capsules of NASA's Mercury, Gemini, and Apollo space projects in the 1960s. Although hidden (for reasons of racism), they nevertheless played a critical role within the engineering system as a group into which the NASA engineers could cognitively extend to enhance and supersize their engineering work. Like the members of a navigational team on the bridge of a naval ship, these women were one part of a larger interactive cognitive network capable of solving problems in an efficient and timely manner that would be beyond the capacity of a single individual.

It is interesting to consider the impact of the segregation of these women mathematicians into the basement of another building. In addition to the issues of social justice behind this arrangement, the project was negatively impacted by the absence of the cognitive coupling and enhancement involved in more direct interactivity and feedback. Part of the plot of the movie is how this arrangement had to be overcome in order for the cognitive work of the project to be supersized in the ways it could only be with at least one of the women present in the discussions.

SHIPS, SPACESHIPS, AND CHURCHES

These two illustrations—navigating a ship and designing space capsules—are not metaphors about extended cognition but actual examples. However,

---

[4]Merlin Donald, *A Mind So Rare: The Evolution of Human Consciousness* (New York: Norton, 2001), 298.

these scenarios of navigation and space engineering can also be helpful as broader conceptual metaphors for thinking about the extension of our Christian lives within the life of a church and the relationship of our extended lives to the mission of the church. That is, considering these illustrations as broader conceptual metaphors suggests the role of individuals within churches and the power of reciprocal cognitive extensions in enhancing the mission of the church within the reign of God.

We take the ship or the spaceship design project to map onto something about a *local* body of Christ. The body has resources: tools, skills, knowledge, wisdom, and traditions, as well as persons who all have some role to play. Navigating the ship or advancing the design project we liken to the role of the church in participating in the activity of God in the world. All members of the congregation need to form a smoothly functioning network of reciprocal extension focused on becoming a life-giving people of God that participates in God's work in the world. The work on which a congregation focuses is both internal (the life of the congregation) and external (the work of God in the community of which the church is a part).

The resources (artifacts) available to church bodies are mostly commonplace, and their role in enhancing the life of the body is often ignored. Tools that enhance the life and work of the church might include a building and its furnishings (sanctuary and other spaces), resource materials for preaching and teaching, communication media (from telephone to texts to Facebook), digital presentation media (such as PowerPoint to use in services), musical instruments, meeting rooms, a kitchen, parking lots, child play spaces and equipment, and, of course, money. These tools are available to be utilized by persons in ways that enhance the life of the body.

Persons within the congregation interact with tools and with one another in a manner that (hopefully) supersizes the life and ministry of the congregation and in the process enhances the Christian life of its members. Just as accurate navigation emerges from the interactive work of the persons on the bridge of a ship, or successful spaceship design is the product of the collective mind of many (including the hidden group of mathematicians), a robust life together in a congregation, and effective participation in the work of God in the local community, emerges from the interactive life and work of the members of the congregation using whatever tools and interactive resources are available.

A contrasting metaphor from that of the interactive process of navigation of a ship would be the image of each individual person in their own small boat scurrying around by themselves trying to reach some destination based on their own individual skill and effort. They would be much less likely to find the destination, and, as individuals, of much lesser value if they happen to arrive. Similarly, a lot of time spent in solo engineering work will not result in a complete or adequate space capsule design.

CONGREGATIONS AS BODIES

A different metaphor for the life of the church that is very much like our navigational metaphor is offered by Paul in Romans 12:4-8. Here Paul likens the church and its congregants to a physical human body. In fact, use of the term "body of Christ" to refer to the church is in reference to Paul's body metaphor. We all belong together in the same body, but each has a different place and role in the functioning of the body. As examples of these roles (gifts, abilities), Paul includes prophecy, service, teaching, encouragement, giving, leading, and showing mercy.

Clearly illustrated by this analogy is the notion that the *telos* of the participation of each person is for the body as a whole to be able to work effectively toward some end. Thus, it implicitly argues against the sort of individualism that focuses on personal spirituality. Rather, the emphasis is on how each fits into the network that functions to advance the mission of God's reign. This recognition of the uniqueness of one's gifts is also an argument against a one-size-fits-all ministry model. Different individuals have different gifts and therefore serve different functions important to the whole. Isolated from the context of a smoothly functioning network of reciprocal extension within a group of Christians who are sharing life together, the roles described by Paul have little to offer the mission of manifesting the presence and work of God in the world.

This same metaphor is again taken up by Paul in 1 Corinthians 12:4-31. Here there is even greater emphasis on the inappropriateness of focus on the contributions, roles, or independent spiritual statuses of individuals. Although different parts of the body get greater or lesser attention with respect to on-going activity (e.g., hands vs. feet), they are all part of the same body, contributing in different ways to the person's life. Here even the parts that are weaker or less honorable are touted as of vital importance to the life of the body. The entire passage is focused on the contributions of many individuals within an interactive network of cognitive extension toward the aim of enhancement of the life and work of the body of Christ. Although we can imagine consequent side benefits in the continued formation of participating individuals, the import of these passages is the life and vitality of the whole body.

With respect to our Christian lives, the possibility of cognitive extension and soft coupling with what is available outside of ourselves (tools and artifacts, other persons, and wikis) suggests where more robust Christian living might be found. It also suggests what might be the particular value of networks of extended and dynamically soft-coupled communal Christian life with respect to the reign of God in our local communities. We often suffer from the same delusion as the NASA engineers regarding the distinctness and individuality of their work. By allowing an important part of their work to remain hidden, they were less productive than they needed to be. As the story unfolded, by extension to and incorporation of at least one of these women more directly into the interactive network, the collective mind of the project group was enhanced. So, in the end we raise the question, What remains hidden that, if we were to recognize it and extend our lives into it, could enhance our Christian lives, both corporately and individually?

BIBLIOGRAPHY

Aron, Lewis. *A Meeting of Minds: Mutuality in Psychoanalysis*. Hillsdale, NY: The Analytic Press, 1996.

Balswick, Jack O., Pamela Ebstyne King, and Kevin S. Reimer, *The Reciprocating Self: Human Development in Theological Perspective*, 2nd ed. Downers Grove: InterVarsity Press, 2016.

Baumeister, Juan Carlos, Guido Papa, and Francesco Foroni. "Deeper than Skin Deep: The Effect of Botulinum Toxin-A on Emotion Process." *Toxicon* 118 (2016): 86-90. https://www.sciencedirect.com/science/article/pii/S0041010116301179?via%3Dihub.

Bellah, Robert, Richard Madsen, William M. Sullivan, Ann Swidler, and Steven M. Tipton. *Habits of the Heart: Individualism and Commitments in American Life*. New York: Harper & Row, 1985.

Benjamin, Jessica. "Beyond Doer and Done To: An Intersubjective View of Thirdness." *The Psychoanalytic Quarterly* 73 (2004): 4-56.

Bolsinger, Tod E. *It Takes a Church to Raise a Christian: How the Community of God Transforms Lives*. Grand Rapids: Brazos Press, 2004.

Bonhoeffer, Dietrich. *Life Together: The Classic Exploration of Faith in Community*. New York: Harper & Row, 1954.

Borg, Marcus. *The God We Never Knew: Beyond Dogmatic Religion to a More Authentic Contemporary Faith*. San Francisco: HarperCollins, 2009.

Broderick, Carlfred B. *Understanding Family Process: Basics of Family Systems Theory*. Thousand Oaks, CA: Sage Publications, 1993.

Brown, Warren S. "Resonance: A Model for Relating Science, Psychology, and Faith." *Journal of Psychology and Christianity* 23 (2004): 110-20.

———. "The Brain, Religion, and Baseball: Comments on the Potential for a Neurology of Religion." In *Where God and Science Meet: How Brain and Evolutionary Studies Alter Our Understanding of Religion; Volume II: The Neurology of Religious Experience*, edited by Patrick McNamara, 229-44. Westport, CT: Praeger Publishers, 2006.

Brown, Warren S., Sarah D. Marion, and Brad D. Strawn. "Human Relationality, Spiritual Formation, and Wesleyan Communities." In *Wesleyan Theology and Social Science: The Dance of Practical Divinity and Discovery*, edited by M. Kathryn Armistead, Brad D. Strawn, and Ronald W. Wright, 95-112. Cambridge, UK: Cambridge University Press, 2010.

Brown, Warren S., Nancey Murphy, and Newton Malony, eds. *Whatever Happened to the Soul? Scientific and Theological Portraits of Human Nature*. Minneapolis: Fortress Press, 1998.

Brown, Warren S., and Brad D. Strawn. *The Physical Nature of Christian Life: Neuroscience, Psychology, and the Church*. Cambridge, UK: Cambridge University Press, 2012.

Buechler, Sandra. *Still Practicing: The Heartaches and Joys of a Clinical Career*. New York: Routledge, 2012.

Cary, Phillip. *Augustine's Invention of the Inner Self: The Legacy of a Christian Platonist*. Oxford, UK: Oxford University Press, 2000.

Chalmers, David. "Facing Up to the Problem of Consciousness." *Journal of Consciousness Studies* 2, no. 3 (1995): 200-219.

Claiborne, Shane, and Jonathan Wilson-Hartgrove. *Becoming the Answer to Our Prayers: Prayers for Ordinary Radicals*. Downers Grove, IL: InterVarsity Press, 2008.

Clapp, Rodney. *Tortured Wonders: Christian Spirituality for People, Not Angels*. Grand Rapids: Brazos Press, 2004.

Clark, Andy. *Being There: Putting Brain, Body, and World Together Again*. Cambridge, MA: MIT Press, 1997.

———. *Natural Born Cyborgs: Minds, Technologies, and the Future of Human Intelligence*. Oxford, UK: Oxford University Press, 2003.

———. *Supersizing the Mind: Embodiment, Action, and Cognitive Extension*. Oxford, UK: Oxford University Press, 2011.

Clark, Andy, and David Chalmers. "The Extended Mind," *Analysis 58*, no. 1 (1998): 7-19.

Cuffari, Elena. "Keep Meaning in Conversational Coordination." *Frontiers in Psychology* 5 (2014): 1397. https://doi.org/10.3389/fpsyg.2014.01397.

Curtiss, Susan. *Genie: A Psycholinguistic Study of a Modern-Day "Wild Child."* Boston: Academic Press, 1977.

Damasio, Antonio. *The Feeling of What Happens: Body and Emotion in the Making of Consciousness*. New York: Harcourt, 1999.

Dennett, Daniel C. *Consciousness Explained*. Little, NY: Brown & Co., 1991.

Dijkstra, Katinka, Michael P. Kaschak, and Rolf A. Zwaan. "Body Posture Facilitates Retrieval of Autobiographical Memories." *Cognition* 102 (2007): 139-49.

Donald, Merlin. *A Mind So Rare: The Evolution of Human Consciousness*. New York: Norton, 2001.

Dumouchel, Paul. "Emotions and Mimesis." In *Mimesis and Science: Empirical Research on Imitation and the Mimetic Theory of Culture and Religion,* edited by Scott R. Garrels, 75-86. East Lansing, MI: Michigan State University Press, 2011.

Edelman, Gerald, and Giulio Tononi. *Consciousness: How Matter Becomes Imagination*. London: Allen Lane, 2000.

Foster, Richard J. *Celebration of Discipline: The Path to Spiritual Growth*. San Francisco: Harper, 1988.

Gallagher, Shaun. "The Socially Extended Mind." *Cognitive Systems Research* 25-26 (2013): 4-12.

Gleich, James. *Genius: The Life and Science of Richard Feynman.* New York: Pantheon, 1992.

Green, Joel B. *Body, Soul, and Human Life: The Nature of Humanity in the Bible.* Grand Rapids: Baker Academic, 2008.

———, ed. *What About the Soul? Neuroscience and Christian Anthropology.* Nashville: Abingdon Press, 2004.

Greeno, James G. "The Situativity of Knowing, Learning, and Research." *American Psychologist* 53, no. 1 (1998): 5-26.

Halberstadt, Jamin, Piotr Winkielman, Paula M. Niedenthal, and Nathalie Dalle. "Emotional Conception: How Embodied Emotion Concepts Guide Perception and Facial Action." *Psychological Science* 20, no.10 (2009): 1254-61. https://journals.sagepub.com/doi/10.1111/j.1467-9280.2009.02432.x.

Heard, William G. *The Healing Between: A Clinical Guide to Dialogical Psychotherapy.* San Francisco: Jossey-Bass, 1993.

Hefner, Philip, Ann Milliken Pederson, and Susan Barreto. *Our Bodies Are Selves.* Eugene, OR: Cascade Books, 2015.

Hesslow, Germund. "The Current Status of the Simulation Theory of Cognition." *Brain Research* 1428 (2012): 71-79.

Hoffman, Marie T. *Toward Mutual Recognition: Relational Psychoanalysis and the Christian Narrative.* New York: Routledge, 2011.

Hofstadter, Douglas. *I Am a Strange Loop.* New York: Basic Books, 2007.

Hutchins, Edwin. *Cognition in the Wild.* Cambridge, MA: MIT Press, 1995.

Ignatius, Saint. *The Spiritual Exercises of Saint Ignatius.* Translated by George E. Ganss. Chicago: Loyola Press, 1992.

James, William. *Varieties of Religious Experience: A Study in Human Nature.* New York: The Modern Library, 1902.

Jeeves, Malcolm A., and Warren S. Brown. *Neuroscience, Psychology, and Religion: Illusions, Delusions, and Realities about Human Nature.* West Conshohocken, PA: Templeton Foundation Press, 2009.

Jeeves, Malcolm A., and Thomas E. Ludwig. *Psychological Science and Christian Faith: Insights and Enrichments from Constructive Dialogue.* West Conshohocken, PA: Templeton Foundation Press, 2018.

Johnson, Luke Timothy. *The Revelatory Body: Theology as Inductive Art.* Grand Rapids: Eerdmans, 2015.

Johnson, Mark L. *The Meaning of the Body: Aesthetics of Human Understanding.* Chicago: University of Chicago Press, 2007.

Jones, Alan. *Soul Making: The Desert Way of Spirituality,* San Francisco: HarperSanFrancisco, 1989.

Jonker, Peter. *Preaching in Pictures: Using Images for Sermons that Connect.* Nashville: Abingdon Press, 2015.

Juarrero, Alicia. *Dynamics in Action: Intentional Behavior as a Complex System.* Cambridge, MA: MIT Press, 1999.

Kensinger, Elizabeth A., Hae-Yoon Choi, Brendan D. Murray, and Suparna Rajaram. "How Social Interactions Affect Emotional Memory Accuracy: Evidence from Collaborative Retrieval and Social Contagion Paradigms." *Memory & Cognition* 44, no.5 (2016): 706-16. https://doi.org/10.3758/s13421-016-0597-8.

Kerr, Fergus. *Theology After Wittgenstein.* 2nd ed. Oxford, UK: Basil Blackwell Ltd., 1997.

Keysers, Christian. *The Empathic Brain: How the Discovery of Mirror Neurons Changes Our Understanding of Human Nature.* Self-published, Amazon Digital Services, 2011. Kindle.

Kruger, Tillmann H. C., and M. Axel Wollmer. "Depression—An Emerging Indication for Botulinum Toxin Treatment." *Toxicon* 107 (2015): 154-57. https://www.sciencedirect.com /science/article/pii/S0041010115300945?via%3Dihub.

Lakoff, George. "Conceptual Metaphor." In *Cognitive Linguistics: Basic Readings*, edited by Dirk Geeraerts, 189-96. Berlin, Germany: Mouton de Gruyter, 2006.

Lakoff, George, and Mark Johnson. *Philosophy in the Flesh: The Embodied Mind and Its Challenge to Western Thought.* New York: Basic, 1999.

Lakoff, George, and Rafael Nuñez. *Where Mathematics Comes From: How the Embodied Mind Brings Mathematics Into Being.* New York: Basic Books, 2000.

Lewis, Thomas, Fari Amini, and Richard Lannon. *A General Theory of Love.* New York: Random House, 2000.

Lodahl, Michael. "The Cosmological Basis for John Wesley's 'Gradualism.'" *Wesleyan Theological Journal* 32, no.1 (1997): 17-32.

Lowry, Eugene. *The Homiletic Plot: The Sermon as Narrative Art Form.* Louisville, KY: Westminster John Knox, 2001.

MacIntyre, Alasdair. *After Virtue.* 2nd ed. Notre Dame: University of Notre Dame Press, 1981.

———. *Dependent Rational Animals: Why Human Beings Need the Virtues.* Chicago: Open Court, 1999.

MacKay, Donald M. *Behind the Eye.* Cambridge, MA: Basil Blackwell, 1991.

Maddox, Randy L. *Responsible Grace: John Wesley's Practical Theology.* Nashville: Kingswood Books, 1994.

May, Gerald G. *Care of Mind, Care of Spirit: A Psychiatrist Explores Spiritual Direction.* San Francisco: HarperSanFrancisco, 1992.

McAdams, Dan. *The Redemptive Self: Stories Americans Live By.* New York: Oxford University Press, 2005.

McLuhan, Marshall. *Understanding Media: The Extension of Man.* Cambridge, MA: MIT Press, 1994.

Miller, George A. "The Cognitive Revolution: A Historical Perspective." *Trends in Cognitive Sciences* 7, no. 3 (2003): 141-44.

Moll, Rob. *What Your Body Knows About God: How We Are Designed to Connect, Serve and Thrive.* Downers Grove, IL: InterVarsity Press, 2014.

Murphy, Nancey. *Bodies and Souls, or Spirited Bodies?* Cambridge, UK: Cambridge Press, 2006.

Murphy, Nancey, and Warren S. Brown. *Did My Neurons Make Me Do It? Philosophical and Neurobiological Perspectives on Moral Responsibility and Free Will.* Oxford, UK: Oxford University Press, 2007.

Newbigin, Lesslie. *The Gospel in a Pluralist Society.* Grand Rapids: Eerdmans, 1989.

Nijhof, Annabel D., and Roel M. Willems. "Simulating Fiction: Individual Differences in Literature Comprehension Revealed with fMRI." *PLoS One* 10, no. 2 (2015): e0116492. https://doi.org/10.1371/journal.pone.0116492.

Orange, Donna M., George A. Atwood, and Robert D. Stolorow. *Working Intersubjectively: Contextualism in Psychoanalytic Practice.* Hillsdale, NJ: The Analytic Press, 1997.

Owens, Tara M. *Embracing the Body: Finding God in Our Flesh and Bones.* Downers Grove, IL: InterVarsity Press, 2015.

Paulsell, Stephanie. *Honoring the Body: Meditations on a Christian Practice.* San Francisco: Jossey-Bass, 2002.

Pederson, Brent. *Created to Worship: God's Invitation to Become Fully Human.* Kansas City, MO: Beacon Hill Press, 2012.

Proffitt, Dennis R. "Embodied Perception and the Economy of Action." *Perspectives on Psychological Science* 1, no. 2 (2006): 110-22.

Quartz, Steven, and Terrence J. Sejnowski. *Liars, Lovers, and Heroes: What the New Brain Science Reveals About How We Become Who We Are.* New York: William Morrow, 2003.

Rajaram, Suparna, and Luciane P. Pereira-Pasarin. "Collaborative Memory: Cognitive Research and Theory." In *Perspectives on Psychological Science* 5, no. 6 (2010): 649-63. https://doi.org/10.1177/1745691610388763.

Renovaré. "Spiritual Formation." https://renovare.org/about/ideas/spiritual-formation.

Richards, E. Randolph, and Brandon J. O'Brien. *Misreading Scripture with Western Eyes: Removing Cultural Blinders to Better Understand the Bible.* Downers Grove, IL: InterVarsity Press, 2012.

Sandage, Steven J., and Jeannine K. Brown. *Relational Integration of Psychology and Christian Theology: Theory, Research, and Practice.* New York: Routledge, 2018.

Scorgie, Glen. "Overview of Christian Spirituality." In *Dictionary of Christian Spirituality*, edited by Glen Scorgie, 27-33. Grand Rapids: Zondervan, 2011.

Senghas, Ann, Sotaro Kita, and Asli Özyürek. "Children Creating Core Properties of Language: Evidence from an Emerging Sign Language in Nicaragua." *Science* 305 (2004): 1779-82.

Shapiro, Fred R. *The Yale Book of Quotations.* New Haven, CT: Yale University Press, 2006.

Shirky, Clay. *Cognitive Surplus: Creativity and Generosity in a Connected Age.* New York: Penguin Press, 2010.

Speer, Nicole K., Jeremy R. Reynolds, Khena M. Swallow, and Jeffery M. Zacks. "Reading Stories Activates Neural Representations of Visual and Motor Experiences." *Psychological Science* 20 (2009): 989-99. https://doi.org/10.1111/j.1467-9280.2009.02397.x.

Strawn, Brad D., Ron Wright, and Paul Jones. "Tradition-Based Integration: Illuminating the Stories and Practices That Shape Our Integrative Imaginations." *Journal of Psychology & Christianity* 33, no. 4 (2014): 300-310.

Sutton, John, Celia B. Harris, Paul G. Keil, and Amanda J. Barnier. "The Psychology of Memory, Extended Cognition, and Socially Distributed Remembering." *Phenomenology and Cognitive Science* 9 (2010): 521-60. https://doi.org/10.1007/s11097-010-9182-y.

Taylor, Charles. *Sources of the Self: The Making of Modern Identity*. Cambridge, MA: Harvard University Press, 1989.

Teske, John A. "From Embodied to Extended Cognition." *Zygon* 48 (2013): 759-87.

Thomas, Owen C. *Christian Life and Practice: Anglican Essays*. Eugene, OR: Wipf & Stock, 2009.

———. "Interiority and Christian Spirituality." *Journal of Religion* 80, no. 1 (2000): 41-60.

Tribble, Evelyn. "Distributing Cognition in the Globe." *Shakespeare Quarterly* 56 (2005): 135-55.

Van Order, Guy C., John G. Holden, and Michael T. Turvey. "Self-Organization of Cognitive Performance." *Journal of Experimental Psychology* 132 (2003): 331-50.

Vygotsky, Lev S. *The Genesis of Higher Mental Functions*. Vol. 4, *The History of the Development of Higher Mental Functions*, edited by Robert W. Rieber. New York: Plennum, 1987.

Welker, Michael. "We Live Deeper than We Think: The Genius of Schleiermacher's Earliest Ethics." *Theology Today* 56 (1999): 169-79.

Willard, Dallas. *Renovation of the Heart: Putting on the Character of Christ*. Colorado Springs: NavPress, 2002.

Wilson, Jonathan R. *Why Church Matters: Worship, Ministry, and Mission in Practice*. Grand Rapids: Brazos Press, 2007.

Wright, N. T. *After You Believe: Why Christian Character Matters*. New York: HarperCollins, 2010.

Wright, Ron, Paul Jones, and Brad Strawn. "Tradition-Based Integration." In *Christianity & Psychoanalysis: A New Conversation*, edited by Earl D. Bland and Brad D. Strawn, 37-54. Downers Grove, IL: InterVarsity Press, 2014.

Wynkoop, Mildred Bangs. *Foundations of Wesleyan-Arminian Theology*. Kansas City, MO: Beacon Hill Press, 1967.

Yalom, Irvin. *The Theory and Practice of Group Psychotherapy*. 3rd ed. New York: Basic Books, 1985.

NAME INDEX

SUBJECT INDEX

SCRIPTURE INDEX